THE COMPLETE LIBRARY SKILLS – Grade 3

By
Linda Turrell

Cover and Inside Illustrations By
Darcy Myers

Publishers
T.S. Denison & Company, Inc.
Minneapolis, Minnesota 55431

Standard Book Number: 513-02210-4
The Complete Library Skills—Grade 3
Copyright © 1994 by T.S. Denison & Co., Inc.
9601 Newton Avenue South
Minneapolis, Minnesota 55431

Printed in the USA

CONTENTS

WELCOMING THIRD-GRADERS TO THE LIBRARY

Third grade children will become responsible users of the library as they become more independent in using the library and in following library rules relating to acceptable library behavior and the care of books and materials. Before beginning your third grade library program, discuss basic rules of library citizenship as seen in the list below.

Library Citizenship

Keep books in a plastic bag when transporting them to or from the library so that pages will not wrinkle or curl if exposed to moisture.

Use a bookmark rather than bending the corner of a page or leaving the book open flat on its face.

Keep books out of the reach of babies or very young children.

Wash hands before reading a book, otherwise the pages may become sticky or smeared.

Turn pages carefully so they won't tear or wrinkle.

Return books on time so that other children can enjoy them.

In addition to the above you may also want to discuss topics such as honesty in reporting book damage (explain that children should not try to fix a book at home—the library has special "book doctors" to repair damage), the cost of some children's books, and the concept of taxes (which pay for the library books and make them public property).

GRADE THREE BOOKMARKS/ LIBRARY READING INCENTIVES

NAME _____

WHO IS AN AUTHOR?

An author is someone who writes books for others to read. Authors sometimes write about memories from their own childhood, or perhaps they might write stories of make-believe. Many authors write books because they are interested in a certain topic such as space, history, weather, or art.

Authors often do more than write books. Some also teach, some are mothers or fathers, and some are children. If you have ever written a story, then you are an author too!

Make a list of some of your favorite authors.	Would you like to be an author? Why?

(Use the library to help you.)

NAME _____

WHO IS AN ILLUSTRATOR?

An illustrator is someone who adds pictures or drawings to the words an author writes. An illustrator helps the words come alive and also helps the reader better understand what he or she is reading. Illustrators can use paint, chalk, pencils, charcoal, markers, crayons, or even construction paper or crepe paper to illustrate a book. If you have ever used any of these things to design something you have written, then you have been an illustrator.

(Use the library to help you.)

Make a list of some of your favorite illustrators.	Would you like to be an illustrator? Why?

THE CALDECOTT AWARD

The Caldecott Award is given annually to the illustrator of the most distinguished American picture book for children published during the preceding year. The award is named for Randolph Caldecott, the famous English artist and illustrator of books for children. One of the requirements for the award is that the artist be either a citizen or a resident of the United States. Daniel Melcher is the donor of the medal which was originally given by his father, Frederic Melcher. The award is administered and presented by the Association for Library Service to Children—a division of the American Library Association.

The first award was given in 1938 to Dorothy Lathrop for the illustrations in *Animals of the Bible*. Until 1958, the award could not be given to an artist the second time without the unanimous vote of the committee, but in that year the ruling was rescinded. Robert McCloskey was given the award the second time for *Time of Wonder*. Since then, a number of artists have been recipients of the award more than once.

But there are always books with outstanding illustrations that do not become winners. The selection committee may, and usually does, choose Honor Books—other fine picture books that have been serious contenders for the medal.

CALDECOTT ACTIVITIES

- Create a display of Caldecott books in the library. The display should be accessible for the children to look at.

- Make a classroom chart displaying the titles of Caldecott books read by the third grade children.

- Have the children pretend they are the Association for Library Service to Children, and it is their job to choose a new Caldecott winner. Have the children vote for the new winner. They may also wish to choose new Honor Books.

CALDECOTT AWARD WINNERS AND HONOR BOOKS

1938-*Animals of the Bible*
    Illustrated by Dorothy Lathrop
        Honor Books:
Seven Simeons. Boris Artzybasheff.
Four and Twenty Blackbirds. Robert Lawson

1939-*Mei Li*
    Illustrated by Thomas Handforth
        Honor Books:
The Forest Pool. Laura Adams Armer
Wee Gillis. Robert Lawson
Snow White and the Seven Dwarfs. Wanda
    Gag
Barkis. Clare Turlay Newberry
Andy and the Lion. James Daugherty

1940-*Abraham Lincoln*
    Illustrated by Ingri and Edgar Parin
            D'Aulaire
        Honor Books:
Cock-a-Doodle-Doo. Berta and Elmer Hader
Madeline. Ludwig Bemelmans
The Ageless Story. Lauren Ford

1941-*They Were Strong and Good*
    Illustrated by Robert Lawson
        Honor Books:
April's Kittens. Clare Turlay Newberry

1942-*Make Way for Ducklings*
    Illustrated by Robert McCloskey
        Honor Books:
An American ABC. Maud and Miska
    Petersham
In My Mother's House. Velino Herrera
Paddle-to-the-Sea. Holling Clancy Holling
Nothing at All. Wanda Gag

1943-*The Little House*
    Illustrated by Virginia Lee Burton
        Honor Books:
Dash and Dart. Mary and Conrad Buff
Marshmallow. Clare Turlay Newberry

1944-*Many Moons*
    Illustrated by Louis Slobodkin
        Honor Books:
Small Rain. Elizabeth Orton Jones
Pierre Pidgeon. Arnold E. Bare
Good-Luck Horse. Plato Chan
The Mighty Hunter. Berta and Elmer Hader
A Child's Good Night Book. Jean Charlot

1945-*Prayer for a Child*
    Illustrated by Elizabeth Orton Jones
        Honor Books:
Mother Goose. Tasha Tudor
In The Forest. Marie Hall Ets
Yonie Wondernose. Marguerite de Angeli
The Christmas Anna Angel. Kate Seredy

1946-*The Rooster Crows*
    Illustrated by Maud and Miska Petersham
        Honor Books:
Little Lost Lamb. Leonard Weisgard
Sing Mother Goose. Marjorie Torrey
*My Mother is the Most Beautiful Woman in
    the World.* Ruth C. Gannett
You Can Write Chinese. Kurt Weise

1947-*The Little Island*
    Illustrated by Leonard Weisgard
        Honor Books:
Rain Drop Splash. Leonard Weisgard
The Boats on the River. Jay Hyde Barnum
Timothy Turtle. Tony Palazzo
Pedro, the Angel of Olver Street. Leo Politi
Sing in Praise. Marjorie Torrey

1948-*White Snow, Bright Snow*
    Illustrated by Roger Duvoisin
        Honor Books:
Stone Soup. Marcia Brown
McElligot's Pool. Theodor S. Geisel
Bambino the Clown. George Schreiber
Roger and the Fox. Hildegard Woodward
Song of Robin Hood. Virginia Lee Burton

1949-*The Big Snow*
    Illustrated by Berta and Elmer Hader
        Honor Books:
    Blueberries for Sal. Robert McCloskey
    All Around Town. Helen Stone
    Juanita. Leo Politi
    Fish in the Air. Kurt Weise

1950-*Song of the Swallows*
    Illustrated by Leo Politi
        Honor Books:
    America's Ethan Allen. Lynd Ward
    The Wild Birthday Cake. Hildegard
        Woodward
    The Happy Day. Marc Simont
    Henry-Fisherman. Marcia Brown
    Bartholomew and the Oobleck. Theodor S.
        Geisel

1951-*The Egg Tree*
    Illustrated by Katherine Milhous
        Honor Books:
    Dick Whittington and His Cat. Marcia Brown
    The Two Reds. Nicolas Mordvinoff
    If I Ran The Zoo. Theodor S. Geisel
    T-Bone,theBaby-Sitter. Clare Turlay
        Newberry
    The Most Wonderful Doll in the World. Helen
        Stone

1952-*Finders Keepers*
    Illustrated by Nicolas Mordvinoff
        Honor Books:
    Mr. T.W. Anthony Woo. Marie Hall Ets
    Skipper John's Cook. Marcia Brown
    All Falling Down. Margaret B. Graham
    Bear Party. William Pene Du Bois
    Feather Mountain. Elizabeth Olds

1953-*The Biggest Bear*
    Illustrated by Lynd Ward
        Honor Books:
    Puss in Boots. Marcia Brown
    One Morning in Maine. Robert McCloskey
    Ape in a Cape. Fritz Eichenberg
    The Storm Book. Margaret B. Graham
    Five Little Monkeys. Juliet Kepes

1954-*Madeleine's Rescue*
    Illustrated by Ludwig Bemelmans
        Honor Books:
    Journey Cake, Ho! Robert McCloskey
    When Will the World Be Mine? Jean Charlot
    The Steadfast Tin Soldier. Marcia Brown
    A Very Special House. Maurice Sendak
    Green Eyes. Abe Birnbaum

1955-*Cinderella, or the Little Glass Slipper*
    Illustrated by Marcia Brown
        Honor Books:
    Book of Nursery and Mother Goose Rhymes.
        Marguerite de Angeli
    Wheel on the Chimney. Tibor Gergely
    The Thanksgiving Story. Helen Sewell

1956-*Frog Went A-Courtin'*
    Illustrated by Feodor Rojankovsky
        Honor Books:
    Play with Me. Marie Hall Ets
    Crow Boy. Jun Iwamatsu

1957-*A Tree is Nice*
    Illustrated by Marc Simont
        Honor Books:
    Mr. Penny's Race Horse. Marie Hall Ets
    1 is One. Tasha Tudor
    Anatole. Paul Galdone
    Gillespie and the Guards. James Daugherty
    Lion. William Pene Du Bois

1958-*Time of Wonder*
    Illustrated by Robert McCloskey
        Honor Books:
    Fly High. Don Freeman
    Anatole and the Cat. Paul Galdone

1959-*Chanticleer and the Fox*
    Illustrated by Barbara Cooney
        Honor Books:
    The House that Jack Built. Antonio Frasconi
    What Do You Say, Dear? Maurice Sendak
    Umbrella. Jun Iwamatsu

1960-*Nine Days to Christmas*
    Illustrated by Marie Hall Ets
        Honor Books:
    House from the Sea. Adrienne Adams
    Moon Jumpers. Maurice Sendak

1961-*Baboushka and the Three Kings*
Illustrated by Nicolas Sidjakov
Honor Books:
Inch by Inch. Leo Lionni

1962-*Once a Mouse . . .*
Illustrated by Marcia Brown
Honor Books:
The Fox that Went Out on a Chilly Night.
Peter Spier
Little Bear's Visit. Maurice Sendak
The Day We Saw the Sun Come Up. Adrienne
Adams

1963-*The Snowy Day*
Illustrated by Ezra Jack Keats
Honor Books:
The Sun is a Golden Earing. Bernarda Bryson
Mr. Rabbit and the Lovely Present. Maurice
Sendak

1964-*Where the Wild Things Are*
Illustrated by Maurice Sendak
Honor Books:
Swimmy. Leo Lionni
All in the Morning Early. Evaline Ness
Mother Goose and Nursery Rhymes. Philip
Reed

1965-*May I Bring a Friend?*
Illustrated by Beni Montresor
Honor Books:
Rain Makes Applesauce. Marvin Bileck
The Wave. Blair Lent
A Pocketful of Cricket. Evaline Ness

1966-*Always Room for One More*
Illustrated by Nonny Hogrogian
Honor Books:
Hide and Seek Fog. Roger Duvoisin
Just Me. Marie Hall Ets
Tom Tit Tot. Evaline Ness

1967-*Sam, Bangs, and Moonshine*
Illustrated by Evaline Ness
Honor Books:
One Wide River to Cross. Ed Emberley

1968-*Drummer Hoff*
Illustrated by Ed Emberley
Honor Books:
Frederick. Leo Lionni
The Seashore Story. Jun Iwamatsu
The Emperor and the Kite. Ed Young

1969-*The Fool of the World and the Flying Ship*
Illustrated by Uri Shulevitz
Honor Books:
Why the Sun and the Moon Live in the Sky.
Blair Lent

1970-*Sylvester and the Magic Pebble*
Illustrated by William Steig
Honor Books:
Goggles! Ezra Jack Keats
Alexander and the Wind-Up Mouse. Leo
Lionni
Pop Corn and Ma Goodness. Robert Andrew
Parker
Thy Friend, Obadiah. Brinton Turkle
The Judge. Margot Zemach

1971-*A Story, A Story*
Illustrated by Gail E. Haley
Honor Books:
The Angry Moon. Blair Lent
Frog and Toad are Friends. Arnold Lobel
In the Night Kitchen. Maurice Sendak

1972-*One Fine Day*
Illustrated by Nonny Hogrogian
Honor Books:
If All the Seas Were One Sea. Janina
Domanska
Moja Means One: Swahili Counting Book.
Tom Feelings
Hildilid's Night. Arnold Lobel

1973-*The Funny Little Woman*
Illustrated by Blair Lent
Honor Books:
Anansi the Spider. Gerald McDermott
Why Clay Sings. Tom Bahti
Hosie's Alphabet. Leonard Baskin
Snow White and the Seven Dwarfs. Nancy
Ekholm Burkert

1974-*Duffy and the Devil*
    Illustrated by Margot Zemach
        Honor Books:
    Three Jovial Huntsmen. Susan Jeffers
    Catheral: The Story of Its Construction. David
        Macaulay

1975-*Arrow to the Sun*
    Illustrated by Gerald McDermott
        Honor Books:
    Jambo Means Hello. Tom Feelings

1976-*Why Mosquitoes Buzz in People's Ears*
    Illustrated by Leo and Diane Dillon
        Honor Books:
    The Desert is Theirs. Peter Parnall
    Strega Nona. Tomie de Paola

1977-*Ashanti to Zulu: African Traditions*
    Illustrated by Leo and Diane Dillon
        Honor Books:
    Fish for Supper. M.B. Goffstein
    The Contest. Nonny Hogrogian
    The Golem. Beverly McDermott
    Hawk, I'm Your Brother. Peter Parnall
    The Amazing Bone. William Steig

1978-*Noah's Ark*
    Illustrated by Peter Spier
        Honor Books:
    Castle. David Macaulay
    It Could Always be Worse. Margot Zembach

1979-*The Girl Who Loved Wild Horses*
    Illustrated by Paul Goble
        Honor Books:
    Freight Train. Donald Crews
    The Way To Start a Day. Peter Parnall

1980-*Ox-Cart Man*
    Illustrated by Barbara Cooney
        Honor Books:
    Ben's Trumpet. Rachel Isadora
    The Treasure. Uri Schulevitz
    The Garden of Abdul Gasazi. Chris Van
        Allsburg

1981-*Fables*
    Illustrated by Arnold Lobel
        Honor Books:
    The Grey Lady and the Strawberry Snatcher.
        Molly Bang
    Truck. Donald Crews
    Mice Twice. Joseph Low

1982-*Jumanji*
    Illustrated by Chris Van Allsburg
        Honor Books:
    Where the Buffaloes Begin. Stephen Gammell
    On Market Street. Anita Lobel
    Outside Over There. Maurice Sendak
    A Visit to William Blake's Inn. Alice and
        Martin Provensen

1983-*Shadow*
    Illustrated by Marcia Brown
        Honor Books:
    When I Was Young In the Mountains. Diane
        Goode
    A Chair for My Mother. Vera B. Williams

**1984-*The Glorious Flight: Across the Channel
    with Louis Bleriot July 25, 1909***
    Illustrated by Alice and Martin Provensen
        Honor Books:
    Ten, Nine, Eight. Molly Bang
    Little Red Riding Hood. Trina Schart Hyman

1985-*Saint George and the Dragon*
    Illustrated by Trina Schart Hyman
        Honor Books:
    The Story of Jumping Mouse. John Steptoe
    Have You Seen My Duckling? Nancy Tafuri
    Hansel and Gretel. Paul O. Zelinsky

1986-*The Polar Express*
    Illustrated by Chris Van Allsburg
        Honor Books:
    The Relatives Came. Stephen Gammell
    King Bidgood's in the Bathtub. Don Wood

1987-*Hey, Al*
    Illustrated by Richard Egielski
        Honor Books:
    The Village of Round and Square Houses. Ann
        Grifalconi
    Alphabatics. Suse MacDonald
    Rumpelstiltskin. Paul O. Zelinsky

1988-*Owl Moon*
    Illustrated by John Schoenherr
        Honor Books:
    *Mufaro's Beautiful Daughters: An African
        Tale*. John Steptoe

1989-*Song and Dance Man*
    Illustrated by Stephen Gammell
        Honor Books:
    The Boy of the Three-Year Nap. Allen Say
    Free Fall. David Weisner
    Goldilocks and the Three Bears. James
        Marshall
    Mirandy and Brother Wind. Jerry Pinkney

**1990-*Lon Po Po: A Red-Riding Hood Story from
China***
    Illustrated by Ed Young
        Honor Books:
    Bill Peet: An Autobiography. Bill Peet
    Color Zoo. Lois Ehlert
    Hershel and the Hanukkah Goblins. Eric
        Kimmel
    *The Talking Eggs. A Folktale from the
        American South*. Jerry Pinkney

1991-*Black and White*
    Illustrated by David Macaulay
        Honor Books:
    Puss in Boots. Fred Marcellino
    *"More, More, More," Said the Baby: Three
        Love Stories*. Vera B. Williams

1992-*Tuesday*
    Illustrated by David Miesner
        Honor Books:
    Tar Beach. Faith Ringgold

1993-*Mirette on the High Wire*
    Illustrated by Emily Arnold McCully
        Honor Books:
    Seven Blind Mice. Ed Young
    *The Stinky Cheese Man and Other Fairly
        Stupid Tales*. Lane Smith
    Working Cotton. Carole Byard

1994-*Grandfather's Journey*
    Illustrated by Allen Say
        Honor Books:
    Peppe the Lamplighter. Ted Lewin
    *Raven: A Trickster Tale from the Pacific
        Northwest*. Gerald McDermott
    Yo! Yes? Chris Raschka
    Owen. Kevin Henkes

1995-*Smoky Night*
    Illustrated by David Diaz
        Honor Books:
    John Henry. Jerry Pinkney
    Swamp Angel. Paul Zelinksy
    Time Flies. Eric Rohmann

1996-*Officer Buckle and Gloria*
    Illustrated by Peggy Rathman
        Honor Books:
    Alphabet City. Stephen T. Johnson
    The Faithful Friend. Brian Pinkney
    Tops and Bottoms. Janet Stevens
    Zin! Zin! Zin! A Violin. Marjorie Priceman

1997-*Golem*
    Illustrated by David Wisniewski
        Honor Books:
    Hush! A Thai Lullaby. Holly Meade
    The Graphic Alphabet. David Pelletier
    The Paperboy. Dav Pilkey
    Starry Messenger. Peter Sis

THE CALDECOTT MEDAL

Look at the medal displayed on the cover of a Caldecott book.
Try to draw the medal.

Name _____

CALDECOTT CATERPILLAR

Color and cut out the caterpillar.
Write titles of Caldecott books as you read them.

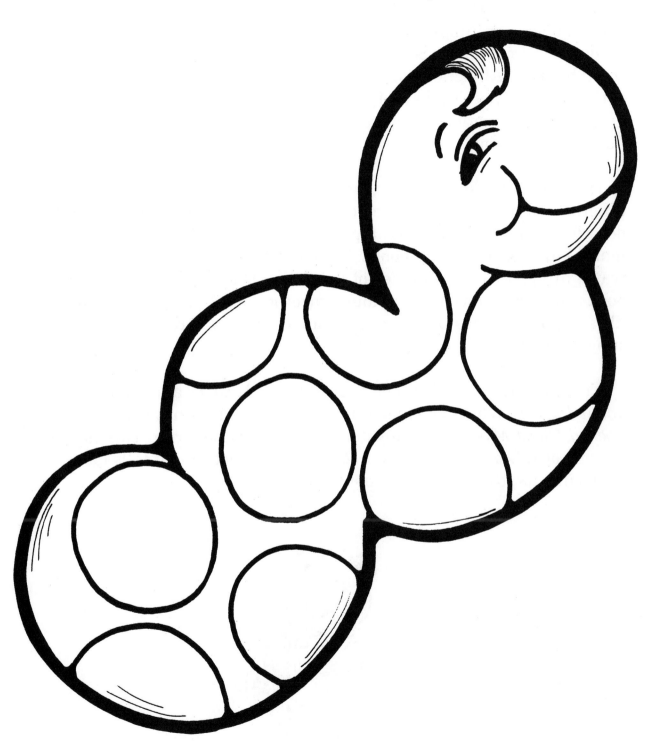

FICTION AND NONFICTION

Fiction and nonfiction are two words used to categorize books. As we have seen in the preceding pages, a fiction book tells a story of people, places, or things that are not true, that is, all fiction books are made-up or imaginary. (Some fiction books, however, seem as if they could be true.) All fiction books are found together in the same area of the library. These books all have a letter "F" on their spine and are arranged alphabetically according to the first two letters of the author's last name.

Nonfiction books, however, usually contain information about different subjects—these types of books are factual, that is, they describe true facts about the topic being written about. There are many kinds of nonfiction books. Books about science, history, and travel are just some examples of nonfiction books. Like the fiction books, all nonfiction books are found together in the same area of the library. These books are arranged numerically according to their subject matter.

Compare the two titles, *The Locked Chest Mystery* and *Learning about Insects*. Which book would tell a story that is not true? *The Locked Chest Mystery* is a mystery book and is not true. This is a fiction book. *Learning about Insects* is about insects and it tells facts about insects, therefore it is a nonfiction book.

FICTION OR NONFICTION

NAME _____

Read the book titles and their descriptions below. Does the book tell an imaginary story? Is the book based on facts? If it is factual, then it is a nonfiction book. Write the word "fiction" or "nonfiction" after each book.

1. *Bugs in Your Backyard* by Pat Beetle is about insects. This book tells about the insects in your backyard.

   _____

2. *The Mystery of the Purple Shoes* by Carla Spy is a detective story. It tells the story of a pair of missing purple shoes.

   _____

3. *Kids Cook!* by John Frypan tells how children can make simple meals.

   _____

4. *The Green Parakeet* by Roger Tweet tells the story of William's first pet. This story is about a boy and his bird.

   _____

5. *How to Choose Your Pet* by Carol Vet tells how to find the pet that is right for you.

   _____

6. *Baking Your Own Bread* by Robert Oven tells how to bake bread.

   _____

FICTION OR NONFICTION

NAME _____

     Read the book titles and their descriptions below. Does the book tell an imaginary story? Is the book based on facts? If it is factual, then it is a nonfiction book. Write the word "fiction" or "nonfiction" after each book.

1. *How to Collect Rocks* by Jason Stone tells how to find rocks and gives step-by-step guidelines for starting your own collection.

    _____

2. *Frogs and Toads* by Beth Rivet tells about the life cycles of these animals.

    _____

3. *To Catch a Blue Starfish* by Teri Sand tells of the adventures of a child at the seashore.

    _____

4. *Cars and Trucks: Their Story* by James Brake. This book tells the history of cars and trucks in America.

    _____

5. *The History of the Kite* by Lynn String tells about the history of the kite and what early kites looked like.

    _____

6. *Can You Hear the Jungle Beasts*? by Raymond Call tells the story of a boy who hears strange jungle sounds in his room.

    _____

FICTION OR NONFICTION

Read the book titles and their descriptions below. Does the book tell a story that is not true or imaginary? If so, then it is a fiction book. Is the book based on facts? If it is, then it is a nonfiction book. Write the word "fiction" or "nonfiction" after each book.

1. *Baby Bumblebee* by Sue Sting tells a story about a bee who gets lost among the flowers.

   _____

2. *The Book of Dogs* by John Spot tells all about dogs.

   _____

3. *How to Write a Report* by Marcia Paper is a step-by-step book on how to write a good report.

   _____

4. *How to Play Baseball* by Roger Base. This book gives all the rules of baseball.

   _____

5. *The Case of the Missing Glove* by John Finger is the story of a missing glove and a hidden treasure.

   _____

6. *My Dog Always Eats Spaghetti* by Jenny Meatball. This is the story of a dog who only eats spaghetti.

   _____

ILLUSTRATE YOUR OWN FICTION BOOK.

Remember to include a title and the author's name on your book cover.

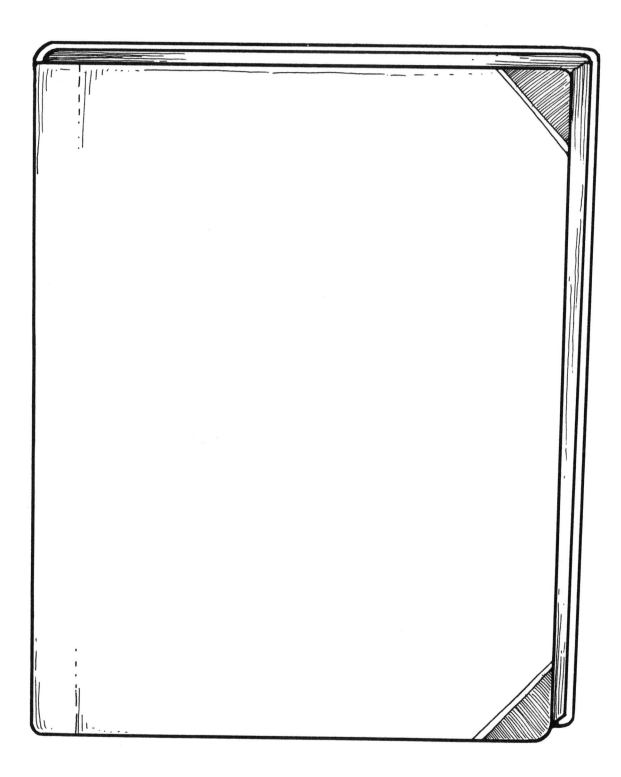

Name _____

ILLUSTRATE YOUR OWN
NONFICTION BOOK.

Remember to include a title and the author's name on your book cover.

NAME _____

FICTION OR NONFICTION?

Many times you can tell if a book is fiction or nonfiction just by reading the title. Read the following book titles and write the word "fiction" or "nonfiction" after each title.

1. *Frogs, Toads, and Other Animals* _____

2. *How to Take Care of Your Puppy* _____

3. *The History of Bicycles* _____

4. *The Life of a Hamster* _____

5. *Baseball for Kids* _____

6. *Mystery of the Fuzzy Hat* _____

7. *All about Bugs* _____

8. *Mystery of the Singing Bird* _____

9. *How to Collect Rocks* _____

10. *A Guide to Mexico* _____

11. *Let's Learn about Sharks!* _____

12. *Dinosaurs of Long Ago* _____

13. *Me, Megan, and the Magic Spell* _____

14. *The Mouse Who Ate the Stars* _____

15. *Six Scary Stories* _____

16. *How to Draw Animals* _____

NAME _____

FICTION OR NONFICTION?

Many times you can tell a book is fiction or nonfiction just by reading the title. Read the following book titles and either write the word "fiction" or "nonfiction" after each title.

1. *Science Experiments You Can Do*   _____

2. *Me and My Teddy Bear*   _____

3. *The Tree That Grew Buttons*   _____

4. *The Complete Book of Insects*   _____

5. *Strange Animals of Australia*   _____

6. *The Book of Planets and Stars*   _____

7. *The Book of Ants and Spiders*   _____

8. *The Mouse Who Laughed at Cats*   _____

9. *Snakes and Reptiles*   _____

10. *The History of the Television*   _____

11. *The Mystery of the Old Clock*   _____

12. *The Cat Lost His Shoes*   _____

13. *Nifty the Clown's Circus Mystery*   _____

14. *Basketball for Kids*   _____

15. *Jacob and the Three Wishes*   _____

16. *Book of Whales*   _____

FICTION CALL NUMBERS

Books have names and "addresses" just like people do. A street address lets people know where someone lives. A **call number** works like a street number—it tells you where to find a book in the library. Street addresses are in numerical order, call numbers are in alphabetical order. A call number is found on the **spine** of the book as well as on the book pocket and the library check-out card inside the book pocket.

If a book is categorized as **fiction**, the book will have a capital letter "F" on its spine. This "F" stands for fiction. A fiction book tells a story and is not based on facts or truth. You will find two letters under the letter "F." These letters are the first two letters of the author's last name. They form the call number of a fiction book. The call number will help you find a book in your library. Let's look at two examples:

Peter Shortcake wrote *Strawberries for Sale*, a fiction book. How do we know it is a fiction book? The capital letter "F" is on the spine. What two letters will be under the "F"? What is Peter's last name? His last name is Shortcake. What are the first two letters of his last name? These letters are "Sh." The call number will look like this:

F
Sh

What about *The Kite and the Tree* by James Cloud? This book is also a fiction book— we can tell by the "F" on the spine. What two letters will be under the "F"? Look at the name James Cloud. What are the first two letters of his last name? They are "Cl." So the call number will look like this:

F
Cl

Name _____

Write the **fiction** call numbers that would appear on books written by the authors below. The first one has been done for you.

1. Brenda Bookmark   F Bo

2. Peter Spine

3. Linda Card

4. Billy Bookend

5. Francis Fiction

6. Barry Bookcover

7. Kelly Catalog

8. Alice Stamp

9. June Loan

10. Beth Shelf

11. Callie Call

12. Michael Mystery

13. Thomas Tale

14. Lyle Title

15. Sally Story

16. William Page

17. Samuel Story

18. Debbie Due

19. Christy Slip

20. Vern Return

Just as addresses are in numerical order on homes so that you can find a specific house, call numbers are in alphabetical order on books so that you can find a specific book. How do you put call numbers in order? Look at the following:

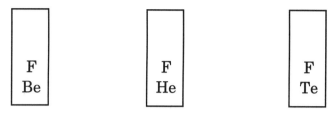

What letter in the alphabet comes first? The letter "B" comes first. What letter comes next? Letter "H." The letter "T" comes next. You do not need to look at the second letters in a call number unless the first letters are the same. Now look at these sample call numbers:

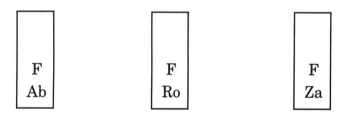

What order do these call numbers go in? Ask yourself what letter comes first in the alphabet, "A," "R," or "Z"? The answer is "A." Then come "R" and "Z." So "Ab" should be first, "Ro" second, and "Za" third. (Remember, when the first letters are different, you do not need to look at the second letters.) Now look at the following:

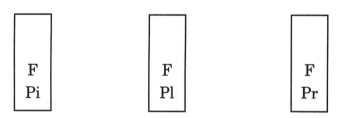

When all of the first letters (the capitals) are the same, then you need to arrange the books in alphabetical order by the second letter of the author's last name. Since the letter "P" is the same first letter of each author's name, you need to look at the second letters: "i," "l," and "r." Now decide the alphabetical order of these letters—then you will have the order that you would find these books on the shelf in a library.

Rearrange the following books so that they are in the correct order. The first one has been done for you. (Remember to include the capital "F" to show that these are fiction books.)

F Ve	F Ce	F Fe		**F Ce**	**F Fe**	**F Ve**

1. | F Lo | F Mo | F Do | | | | |

2. | F Dr | F Mr | F Gr | | | | |

3. | F Ch | F Sh | F Gh | | | | |

4. | F Ma | F Na | F Da | | | | |

5. | F Br | F Tr | F Or | | | | |

Rearrange the following books so that they are in the correct order. The first one has been done for you. (Remember to include the capital "F" to show that these are fiction books.)

F Jo	F Po	F Lo	**F Jo**	**F Lo**	**F Po**

1.

F Gl	F Sl	F Kl

2.

F Mi	F Ri	F Hi

3.

F Qu	F Cu	F Nu

4.

F De	F He	F Me

5.

F Ma	F Za	F Ba

6.

F Fr	F Br	F Gr

NAME _____

PUTTING FICTION
CALL NUMBERS IN ORDER

Look at the books below and decide which order they should be in. Then write "1st," "2nd," or "3rd" under the books to show the correct order. The first one has been done for you.

1. F   F   F
    Ba Za Ra

    _1st_ _3rd_ _2nd_

2. F   F   F
    Ob Eb Ab

    ___ ___ ___

3. F   F   F
    Sn On An

    ___ ___ ___

4. F   F   F
    Ro Zo To

    ___ ___ ___

5. F   F   F
    It At St

    ___ ___ ___

6. F   F   F
    Di Wi Ji

    ___ ___ ___

7. F   F   F
    Br Tr To

    ___ ___ ___

8. F   F   F
    Pi Di Mi

    ___ ___ ___

9. F   F   F
    Mu Lu Pu

    ___ ___ ___

10. F   F   F
    Na Ma Ha

    ___ ___ ___

11. F   F   F
    Gl Sl Bl

    ___ ___ ___

12. F   F   F
    Ch Rh Gh

    ___ ___ ___

NAME _____

PUTTING FICTION
CALL NUMBERS IN ORDER

Look at the books below and decide which order they should be in. Then write "1st," "2nd," or "3rd" under the books to show the correct order. The first one has been done for you.

1. F   F   F
Ra   St   Va

1st   *2nd*   *3rd*

2. F   F   F
Dr   Mr   Gr

___   ___   ___

3. F   F   F
Mo   Co   Lo

___   ___   ___

4. F   F   F
Ze   Ra   To

___   ___   ___

5. F   F   F
Gh   Ut   Ne

___   ___   ___

6. F   F   F
Ma   Ch   Vi

___   ___   ___

7. F   F   F
Jo   Lo   Ye

___   ___   ___

8. F   F   F
Cr   Br   St

___   ___   ___

9. F   F   F
Ov   Ev   Al

___   ___   ___

10. F   F   F
Fl   Ph   Ho

___   ___   ___

11. F   F   F
Gr   Oz   Kr

___   ___   ___

12. F   F   F
Pl   Cl   Bi

___   ___   ___

PUTTING FICTION
CALL NUMBERS IN ORDER

Look at the books below and decide which order they should be in.
Then write "1st," "2nd," or "3rd" under the books to show the correct
order. The first one has been done for you.

1. F   F   F
    Mo   Tr   Ma

    _2nd_ _3rd_ _1st_

2. F   F   F
    Dr   Av   Fr

    ____ ____ ____

3. F   F   F
    Ji   Ju   Jc

    ____ ____ ____

4. F   F   F
    Pa   Pr   Ps

    ____ ____ ____

5. F   F   F
    Wh   Ro   Xy

    ____ ____ ____

6. F   F   F
    At   Ot   Av

    ____ ____ ____

7. F   F   F
    Gr   Tr   Ga

    ____ ____ ____

8. F   F   F
    Tr   Te   Th

    ____ ____ ____

9. F   F   F
    Kl   Mo   Ke

    ____ ____ ____

10. F   F   F
    Rs   Ry   Ro

    ____ ____ ____

11. F   F   F
    Lo   Bo   La

    ____ ____ ____

12. F   F   F
    Ce   Ci   Fe

    ____ ____ ____

NONFICTION CALL NUMBERS

Nonfiction books are found in their own section of the library — they will not be found mixed in with story books. Nonfiction books have information about different subjects, such as trees, space, or dolphins. Folktales, fairy tales, and poetry are also considered nonfiction.

Like the fiction books, nonfiction books also have an "address" on their spine that tells you where to find them in the library. It is easy to tell the difference between a fiction and nonfiction book because the fiction book is marked with letters, and the nonfiction book is marked with letters *and* numbers. This number/letter combination is known as a *Dewey call number*. This number will tell you what section of the library the book is shelved in. The subject of a book will determine its number (see the chart on page 37.) The letters of the Dewey call number are the first two letters of the author's last name.

Example: *The Book of Seashells* by Allen Shore has a call number of:

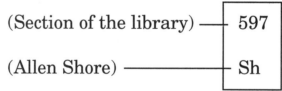

(Section of the library) —— 597

(Allen Shore) —————— Sh

PUTTING NONFICTION CALL NUMBERS ON THE SHELVES

Nonfiction books are arranged on the shelf starting with the lowest call number (000) and work up to the highest call number (999).

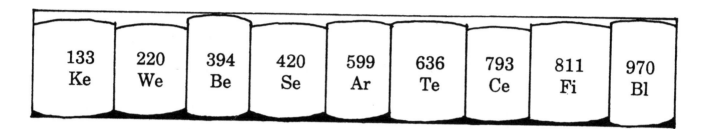

| 133 Ke | 220 We | 394 Be | 420 Se | 599 Ar | 636 Te | 793 Ce | 811 Fi | 970 Bl |

If there is more than one book with the same number, the books with the same number are arranged alphabetically (like fiction books) until a higher number is reached.

| 599 Gr | 599 Zi | 636 Te | 636 Wi | 793 Ce | 793 Mo | 811 Ca | 811 He | 811 Se |

NAME _____

ORDERING DEWEY CALL NUMBERS

Put these Dewey call numbers in order. (Hint: Remember that when the numbers are all different, you do not have to look at the letters. If any of the numbers are the same, you need to look at, and alphabetize the letters.) The first one has been done for you.

1. 400 Ta **2**
2. 800 Bk **4**
3. 900 Br **5**
4. 600 St **3**
5, 300 Ad **1**

1. 400 Wa _____
2. 600 Re _____
3. 500 Al _____
4. 300 Sr _____
5, 200 Be _____

1. 900 De _____
2. 700 Fl _____
3. 500 Ho _____
4. 400 Jo _____
5, 200 Cr _____

---

1. 470 Sr _____
2. 470 Bu _____
3. 450 Fr _____
4. 420 Fl _____
5. 410 Ma _____

1. 850 Th _____
2. 890 Bu _____
3. 890 Ze _____
4. 830 Gu _____
5. 870 Me _____

1. 670 Hu _____
2. 660 To _____
3. 620 Fr _____
4. 620 Op _____
5. 680 Nu _____

NAME _____

ORDERING DEWEY CALL NUMBERS

Put these Dewey call numbers in order. (Hint: Remember that when the numbers are all different, you do not have to look at the letters. If any of the numbers are the same, you need to look at, and alphabetize the letters.) The first one has been done for you.

1.	537 Ke	**5**	1.	964 Ta	_____	1.	757 Br	_____
2.	536 Or	**4**	2.	963 Bk	_____	2.	753 Ab	_____
3.	534 Jo	**2**	3.	968 Br	_____	3.	759 Pe	_____
4.	535 St	**3**	4.	967 St	_____	4.	752 He	_____
5,	533 Tr	**1**	5,	965 Ad	_____	5,	751 Ca	_____

1.	565 Th	_____	1.	565 Br	_____	1.	673 Pa	_____
2.	432 Ki	_____	2.	432 Sh	_____	2.	421 Ch	_____
3.	152 Ei	_____	3.	384 Ca	_____	3.	678 La	_____
4.	384 Ru	_____	4.	962 Je	_____	4.	496 Li	_____
5.	974 Om	_____	5.	410 Zo	_____	5.	527 We	_____

ORDERING DEWEY CALL NUMBERS

Put these Dewey call numbers in order. (Hint: Remember that when the numbers are all different, you do not have to look at the letters. If any of the numbers are the same, you need to look at, and alphabetize the letters.) The first one has been done for you.

1. 575 Ca **3**	1. 650 Ho _____	1. 340 Bo _____
2. 575 Aa **1**	2. 650 Ao _____	2. 340 Be _____
3. 575 Ba **2**	3. 650 Co _____	3. 340 Ba _____
4. 575 Ma **5**	4. 650 Bo _____	4. 340 Bi _____
5, 575 Ha **4**	5, 650 Do _____	5, 340 Bu _____

1. 970 He _____	1. 345 Ab _____	1. 345 Ab _____
2. 970 Ha _____	2. 346 Ao _____	2. 343 Ao _____
3. 970 Hb _____	3. 345 Ai _____	3. 343 Ai _____
4. 970 Ho _____	4. 342 Ab _____	4. 343 Ab _____
5. 970 Hu _____	5. 341 Ab _____	5. 344 Ab _____

Now that you know how to order nonfiction books by their Dewey call number, you will need a chart that will help explain what the number part of the nonfiction call number means. Using this chart you will be able to find a book on whatever subject you want.

DEWEY DECIMAL SYSTEM

The numbers of nonfiction books are based on the Dewey Decimal System created by Melvil Dewey. He decided books should be grouped together according to their subject. There are ten different groups.

000 - 99 — Books with many subjects all in one book, such as: *World Book Encyclopedia, Book of Knowledge;* also books on the newspaper and reporting.

100 - 199 — Books on feelings, and how to study, thoughts and ideas.

200 - 299 — Religion

300 - 399 — Government, laws, folklore, holidays, fairy tales

400 - 499 — English grammar, foreign languages

500 - 599 — Mathematics, astronomy, earth, planets, birds, plants, wild animals

600 - 699 — Satellites, space ships, useful arts, how to make things, care of pets, medicine

700 - 799 — Drawing, photography, painting, music, games, riddles, sports

800 - 899 — Literature, poems, plays, short stories

900 - 999 — Books about countries, geography, travel, biography, history

DEWEY CALL NUMBER SECTIONS

Information about all of the subjects listed below can be found in the nonfiction section of your library. Look at these nonfiction subjects and, using your chart (found on pg. 37), decide which number section of the library you would look in to find more information. The first one has been done for you.

1. Japan   __500 - 599__

2. zebras   _____

3. cat care   _____

4. soccer   _____

5. Swedish folktales   _____

6. Valentine's Day   _____

7. children's encyclopedia   _____

8. love poems   _____

9. French phrases   _____

10. the solar system   _____

11. U.S. History   _____

12. wildflowers   _____

PLACING TITLES IN THE
DEWEY CALL NUMBER SECTIONS

If you need a book about animals, where would you find it in the library? Look at your Dewey Decimal System Chart. Would you find it in the 200 section of the library? No, this is the religion section. If you look on the chart, you can see that the animal books are found in the 500 section of the library. Read the titles below and write the number of the section of the library where you would find each book.

1. Baby Snakes   _____ **500 - 599** _____

2. Historical Boston   _____

3. I Can Play Baseball   _____

4. Math the Easy Way   _____

5. African Folklore   _____

6. Being Catholic   _____

7. Whales: Gentle Giants   _____

8. It's O.K. to Feel Sad   _____

9. Poems of Ireland   _____

10. Learning About Newspapers _____

11. Geography of Iowa   _____

12. How Plants Grow   _____

PLACING TITLES IN THE
DEWEY CALL NUMBER SECTIONS

If you need a book about animals, where would you find it in the library? Look at your Dewey Decimal System Chart. You can see that the animal books are found in the 500 section of the library. Read the titles below and write the number of the section of the library where you would find each book.

1. How to Groom a Dog   _____

2. Book of Prayers   _____

3. Spanish for Travelers   _____

4. Thumbelina   _____

5. Holiday Fun   _____

6. Multiplication Magic   _____

7. Shakespeare: Four Plays   _____

8. Bill Clinton: The Man   _____

9. Reporting the News   _____

10. Today's Space Ships   _____

11. Minnesota History   _____

12. Halloween Decorations   _____

Choose a **nonfiction** book from the library.
1. Write the title on line 1.
2. Write the author's name on line 2.
3. Write the Dewey call numbers on lines 3 and 4.
4. Color an illustration for the cover of the book.

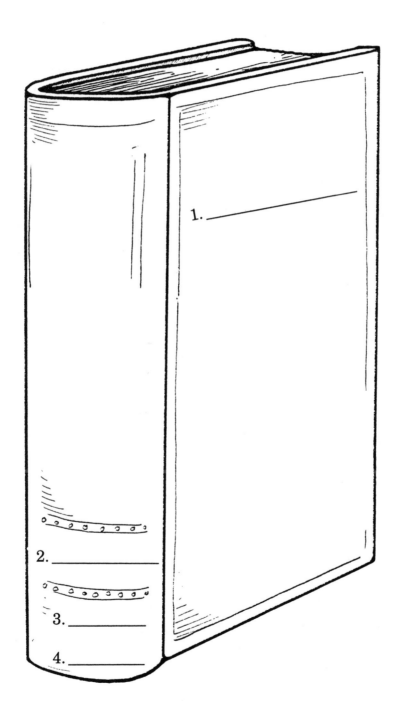

CARD CATALOG

There are clues that help you read a card from the card catalog correctly.

CALL NUMBER – The call number is on the left side of the card all by itself. For nonfiction books, the call number has both numbers and letters. For fiction books, the call number has only letters. The call number tells you where the book is placed on the shelf. You need to know the call number to find the book.

AUTHOR – The author's name is printed with the last name first, then a comma, then the author's first name.

TITLE – The title is printed with mostly lower case letters and has a period at the end. You need to know the title to find the book on the shelf.

ILLUSTRATOR – The illustrator always comes after the title.

PUBLISHER – The publisher comes next on the card. It always comes before the date.

COPYRIGHT DATE – The copyright date tells the year that the book was published. The copyright date comes after the publisher.

PAGES AND GRADE LEVEL – Other information on the card is clued with an abbreviation. For example, "p" means pages, "illus" means illustration and "Gr." means grade level.

Some cards have an annotation which tells something about what is in the book or what the story is about. This can help you decide if a particular book is the one you want to choose.

CARD CATALOG DRAWERS

Using the Card Catalog Drawers.

How do you find the book you need? Think of a time you needed a friend's address or telephone number. You went to the telephone book which has the names and addresses of many people. The telephone book is a collection of information.

The *card catalog* works much the same way. It too is a collection of information and holds a card for every book in your library. **Each book has three cards in the card catalog: the author, the subject, and the title card.** You will find the same information on all three cards, but the first line of each card is different.

- The title card begins with the title.

- The author card begins with the author's name.

- The first line of the subject card is the subject of the book.

Why have all three cards? If you know that the title of a specific book about dinosaurs is called *Learn About Dinosaurs*, and you do not know the author, you would look under the *title* section of the card catalog in the "L" drawer.

Name _____

AUTHOR DRAWER

Author A–D	Author I–J	Author O–P	Author U–V
Author E–F	Author K–L	Author Q–R	Author W–X
Author G–H	Author M–N	Author S–T	Author Y–Z

Which drawer would the following authors' names be found in?

1. Barbara Cooney   _A–D_   11. Maurice Sendak   _____

2. Leo Lionni   _____   12. Peter Spier   _____

3. Evaline Ness   _____   13. Ed Young   _____

4. Ludwig Bemelmans   _____   14. Robert McCloskey   _____

5. Wanda Gag   _____   15. Stephen Gammell   _____

6. David Macaulay   _____   16. Fred Marcellino   _____

7. Vera B. Williams   _____   17. David Wiesner   _____

8. Paul Goble   _____   18. Donald Crews   _____

9. Sid Fleischman   _____   19. Molly Bang   _____

10. John Schoenherr   _____   20. Jerry Pinkney   _____

Name _____

Directions: Cut out the names of the authors and paste them in the correct card catalog drawer.

A–E	**J–K**	**P-Q**
F–G	**L–M**	**R-T**
H-I	**N-O**	**U-Z**

Cut out and paste.

Theodor S. Geisel	Maud & Miska Petersham	James Marshall
Paul O. Zelinsky	Ezra Jack Keats	Trina Schart Hyman
Evaline Ness	John Steptoe	Marvin Bileck

CATALOG CARD—Author

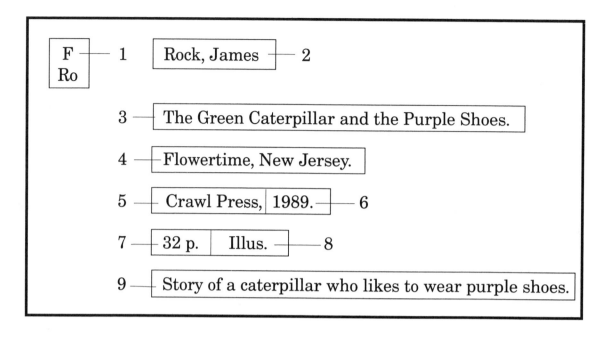

1. ***Call Number*—**   F   This is where you find the
                           Ro   book in the library.

2. ***Author*—** This is the author's name.

3. ***Title*—**This is the title of the book.

4. ***Place of Publication*—**This is where the book was made.

5. ***Publisher*—**This is who made the book.

6. ***Copyright Date*—**This is the birthdate of the book. It is when the book came to be.

7. ***Pages*—**This number tells you how many pages are in the book.

8. ***Illustrations*—**This tells you if the book has pictures.

9. ***Story (or Annotation)*—**This explains the content of the book.

CATALOG CARD—Author

The author's card has the author's name on the very first line. Let's look at an author card.

F   Rock, Pete
Ro

The Dinosaur Who Came to Dinner.

Rockville, New Jersey: Stone Press, 1989.

32 p. Illus.

The story of a dinosaur who came to dinner.

1. Dinosaurs   I. Title   II. Author

Answer these questions.

1. What is the call number? _____

2. What is the title? _____

3. What is the author's name? _____

4. Where was the book made? _____

5. Who published the book? That is who made the book? _____

6. What is the copyright date of the book? _____

7. How many pages are in this book? _____

8. Is the book illustrated? Are there pictures? _____

9. What is this book about? _____

CATALOG CARD—Author

F   Flowers, Peter
Fl

Bumble Cat.

Pollentown, New York: Flower Press, 1989.

64 p. Illus.

Story of a bumble cat. He needs glasses.

1. Cats   I. Title   II. Author

Read these question. Use the card to answer these questions.

1. What is the call number? _____

2. What is the title? _____

3. Who is the author? _____

4. Where was the book published? _____

5. Who made the book? _____

6. What is the copyright date of the book? _____

7. Is the book illustrated? _____

8. What is the book about? _____

9. Is this a fiction book? _____

10. How many pages does this book have? _____

WRITE YOUR OWN
AUTHOR CATALOG CARD

Pick a book of your choice to fill in the blanks.

Call number

Author

Title

Place of Publication, Publisher, Copyright Date

Pages

Illustrated or not

Sentence about what the book is about.

TITLE DRAWER

Title A–E	Title J–K	Title P–Q
Title F–G	Title L–M	Title R–T
Title H–I	Title N–O	Title U–Z

Do you see that each drawer has the word "title" on it? Under the word title are the letters that are in each drawer. Look at the first drawer. These titles begin with A, B, C, D, and E. Look at drawer two. These titles begin with F and G.

Let's say you want to find the card for *Apples for Alligators*. What drawer do you check? Check drawer A–E because the letter A is in this box.

TITLE DRAWER

Title A–D	Title I–J	Title O–P	Title U–V
Title E–F	Title K–L	Title Q–R	Title W–X
Title G–H	Title M–N	Title S–T	Title Y–Z

Which drawer would the following titles be found in?
Write the letters.

1. *The Missing Goldfish Mystery*   _____

2. *Silly Jokes for Kids*   _____

3. *Baseball and Other Sports*   _____

4. *Learning French*   _____

5. *Mystery of the Lost Treasure*   _____

6. *Kites! Kites! Kites!*   _____

7. *Questions and Science*   _____

8. *Eggs and Cooking*   _____

9. *The Happy Blue Frog*   _____

10. *Monkeys and Mice*   _____

TITLE DRAWER

Title A–D	Title I–J	Title O–P	Title U–V
Title E–F	Title K–L	Title Q–R	Title W–X
Title G–H	Title M–N	Title S–T	Title Y–Z

Which drawer would the following titles be found in?
Write the letters.

1. *Airplanes* _____

2. *Tigers in the Wild* _____

3. *Elephants in the Jungle* _____

4. *James and the Missing Key* _____

5. *Sports for Children* _____

6. *Funny Faces* _____

7. *The Beagle's Bone* _____

8. *Michael the Marvelous Mouse* _____

9. *Gerbils* _____

10. *Stars* _____

TITLE DRAWER

Title A–D	Title I–J	Title O–P	Title U–V
Title E–F	Title K–L	Title Q–R	Title W–X
Title G–H	Title M–N	Title S–T	Title Y–Z

Which drawer would the following titles be found in?
Write the letters.

1. *Horses* _____

2. *Stop Watching the Goldfish!* _____

3. *The Orange is Missing* _____

4. *Mystery of the Old Shoe* _____

5. *Messy Maxwell* _____

6. *Wendel Lost His Shoe* _____

7. *Dinosaurs and their Tracks* _____

8. *Gorilla in the Garden* _____

9. *Flowers for Fred* _____

10. *Susan the Super Shopper* _____

A–D	I–J	O–P	U–V
E–F	K–L	Q–R	W–X
G–H	M–N	S–T	Y–Z

Cut and paste the titles in the correct drawer.

Song and Dance Man	*A Frog Prince*	*Young Lions*	*Lon Po Po*
If You Give A Moose A Muffin	*Ramona the Pest*	*A Great Bicycle Book*	*The Polar Express*
Ben's Trumpet	*Where the Wild Things Are*	*Noah's Ark*	*Velveteen Rabbit*

CATALOG CARD—Title

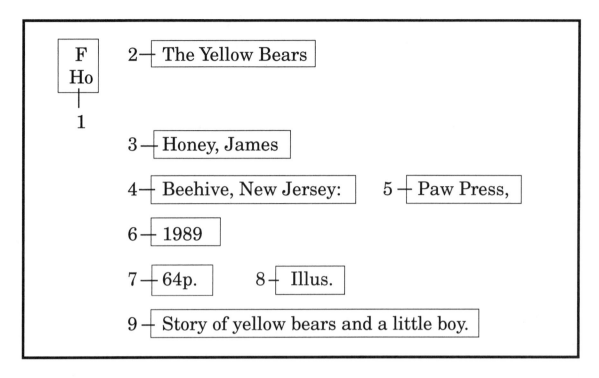

1. **Call Number**—This tells the location of the book in the library.

2. **Title**—This is the title of the book.

3. **Author**—This is the author's name.

4. **Place of publication**—This is where the book was made.

5. **Publisher**—This is who made the book.

6. **Copyright Date**—This is when the book was made.

7. **Pages**—This number tells you how many pages are in the book.

8. **Illustrations**—This tells you if the book has pictures.

9. **Story (or Annotation)**—This tells you what the book is about.

TITLE CARD

The title card begins with the title of the book. Let's look at a sample card.

F Ha	Mystery of the Old Clock Hand, Susan. Mystery of the Old Clock. Numbertown, New York: Watch Press, 1989. 101 p. Illus. Story of the mystery of an old clock. 1. Mystery I. Title II. Author

Read the title card. Answer these questions.

1. What is the title?   _____

2. Who is the publisher? (Who made the book?) _____

3. What is the call number?   _____

4. What is the book about?   _____

5. Where was the book made?   _____

6. What is the author's name?   _____

7. What is the copyright date?   _____

8. How many pages are in the book?   _____

9. Is the book illustrated? (Are there pictures?)_____

10. What is the first line of the card?   _____

TITLE CARD

The title card begins with the title of the book. Let's look at a sample card.

F   The Frog
Ho

       Hop, Fred. The Frog.

       Puddle, New York: Skip Press, 1986.

       28 p. Illus.

       Story of a magic frog.

       1. Fiction   I. Title   II. Author

Read the title card. Answer these questions.

1. What is the call number? _____

2. What is the title? _____

3. Who is the author? _____

4. Where was the book published? _____

5. Who made the book? _____

6. What year was the book made (copyright)? _____

7. Is the book illustrated? _____

8. What is the book about? _____

9. Is this a fiction book? _____

10. How many pages does this book have? _____

TITLE CARD

The title card begins with the title of the book. Let's look at a sample card.

F   The Cat with the Purple Shoes
Sk

Sky, Susan. The Cat with the Purple Shoes.

Meow, New Jersey: Kitty Time Press, 1988.

101 p. Illus.

Story of a cat and his adventures in his purple shoes.

1. Fiction—Cats   I. Title   II. Author

Read the title card. Answer these questions.

1. What is the call number? _____

2. What is the title? _____

3. Who is the author? _____

4. Where was the book published? _____

5. Who made the book? _____

6. What is the copyright date? _____

7. Is the book illustrated? _____

8. What is the book about? _____

9. Is this a fiction book? _____

10. How many pages does this book have? _____

WRITE YOUR OWN
TITLE CATALOG CARD

Pick a book of your choice to fill in the blanks.

Call
number

Title

Author and Title

Place of publication, Publisher, Copyright Date

Pages

Illustrated or not

Sentence about what the book is about.

FINDING SUBJECTS IN THE CARD CATALOG

Let's say that you want to use the subject section of the card catalog. You have an idea of where to look, but you do not know exactly how to look. What do you do?

Well, there are many subjects you can check in the card catalog. Let's say that you need a book about making a drawing for your report about insects. Where do you look? You need a picture of a grasshopper. Look at the subject more closely. You can check "drawing insects." You can look in many places.

Let's try another. Let's say that you need a picture of a tiger for your report about wild animals. Where do you look? You can check under "tigers" or else you may have to check under the broader subject category of "wild animals."

Name _____

SUBJECT DRAWER

Subject A–D	Subject I–J	Subject O–P	Subject U–V
Subject E–F	Subject K–L	Subject Q–R	Subject W–X
Subject G–H	Subject M–N	Subject S–T	Subject Y–Z

Which drawer would the following subjects be found in?

1. Ants   **A - D**   11. Bicycles _____

2. Hamsters _____ 12. Cartoons _____

3. Cooking _____ 13. Stars _____

4. Wasps _____ 14. Ladybugs _____

5. Tigers _____ 15. Frogs _____

6. Caterpillars _____ 16. Rocks _____

7. Presidents _____ 17. Snakes _____

8. Baseball _____ 18. Toads _____

9. Cats _____ 19. Dolls _____

10. Fish _____ 20. Zebras _____

FINDING SUBJECTS IN THE CARD CATALOG

Sometimes the subject you want may be under another word in the card catalog. You may need to check the card catalog more than once.

For example, if you need to find out more about taking care of your pet hamster, check under "hamster." *Pet* is your first subject. *Hamster* is your second.

Look at the following subjects. Write each subject under its column: "Solar System," "Pets," "Insects," "Plants," or "Cooking."

Subject Bank

butterfly	moon	goldfish	bud	pies
hamster	seeds	spices	cats	cookies
Earth	leaf	gerbil	dogs	grasshopper
ferns	cactus	treats	spiders	sun
beetle	Jupiter	Mars	ladybug	recipe

Solar System

1. _____
2. _____
3. _____
4. _____
5. _____

Pets

1. _____
2. _____
3. _____
4. _____
5. _____

Insects

1. _____
2. _____
3. _____
4. _____
5. _____

Plants

1. _____
2. _____
3. _____
4. _____
5. _____

Cooking

1. _____
2. _____
3. _____
4. _____
5. _____

FINDING SUBJECTS IN THE CARD CATALOG

Sometimes the subject you want may be under another word in the card catalog. You may need to check the card catalog more than once.

Look at these subjects. Write the *subject* you might find under each topic or word.

Subject Bank

elephant	blackbird	lion	cardinal	tiger
bluejay	bowling	sparrow	deer	hurricane
football	crow	Pluto	storms	volleyball
Saturn	Neptune	clouds	Earth	snow
Venus	swimming	rain	bear	baseball

Weather

1. _____
2. _____
3. _____
4. _____
5. _____

Planets

1. _____
2. _____
3. _____
4. _____
5. _____

Sports

1. _____
2. _____
3. _____
4. _____
5. _____

Birds

1. _____
2. _____
3. _____
4. _____
5. _____

Animals

1. _____
2. _____
3. _____
4. _____
5. _____

FINDING SUBJECTS IN THE CARD CATALOG

Sometimes you need to look under a different subject in the card catalog. Read these subjects. Under what larger category can you find them?

Category Bank

trumpet	heart	Christmas	Halloween	car
bus	drums	catfish	stomach	blood
Valentines	train	muscle	sunfish	salmon
bluegill	flute	Hanukkah	Easter	airplane
brain	boat	trout	violin	tuba

Instruments

1. _____
2. _____
3. _____
4. _____
5. _____

Human Body

1. _____
2. _____
3. _____
4. _____
5. _____

Ways of Travel

1. _____
2. _____
3. _____
4. _____
5. _____

Holidays

1. _____
2. _____
3. _____
4. _____
5. _____

Fish

1. _____
2. _____
3. _____
4. _____
5. _____

CATALOG CARD—Subject

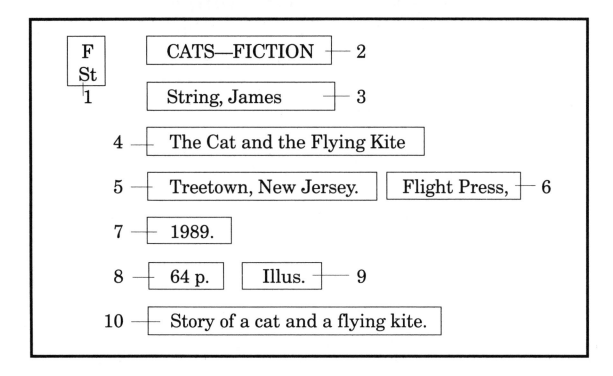

1. **Call Number**—F This is where you find the book in the library.

   St

2. **Subject**—This is the subject of the book.

3. **Author**—This is the author's name.

4. **Title**—This is the title of the book.

5. **Place of publication**—This is where the book was made.

6. **Publisher**—This is who made the book.

7. **Copyright date**—This tells you when the book was made.

8. **Pages**—This number tells you how many pages are in the book.

9. **Illustrations**—This tells you if the book has pictures.

10. **Story (or Annotation)**—This explains the content of the book.

CATALOG CARD—Subject

The subject card has the subject written in capital letters on the very first line of the card. Let's look at a sample card:

F   GERBILS—FICTION
Cl

       Claw, James. My Pet Gerbil Is Turning Green.

       Furrytown, New Jersey.

       Pellet Press, 1989.

       48 p. Illus.

       Story of a gerbil who turns bright green.

       1. Gerbils   I. Title   II. Author

Read the questions. Use the catalog card to find the answer.

1. What is the call number?   _____

2. What is the title?   _____

3. Who is the author?   _____

4. Where was the book published?   _____

5. Who made the book?   _____

6. What is the copyright date?   _____

7. Is the book illustrated?   _____

8. What is the book about?   _____

9. Is this a fiction book?   _____

10. How many pages does the book have?   _____

CATALOG CARD—Subject

The subject card has the subject written in capital letters on the very first line of the card. Let's look at a sample card:

F   MYSTERY STORIES
Fe

     Feather, Sally. Mystery of the Green Parrot.

     Cage, New Jersey.

     Pellet Press, 1988.

     63 p. Illus.

     Story of missing green parrot and a hunk of Swiss cheese.

     1. Fiction I. Subject II. Author

Read these question. Use the card to find the answers.

1. What is the title? _____

2. Where was the book published? _____

3. What is the copyright date? _____

4. What is the book about? _____

5. How many pages does the book have? _____

6. What is the call number? _____

7. Who is the author? _____

8. Who made the book? _____

9. Is the book illustrated? _____

10. Is this a fiction book? _____

THE SUBJECT CARD

The subject card has the subject written in capital letters on the very first line of the card. Let's look at a sample card:

F   TURTLES
Sk
      Sky, Susan. My Pet Turtle Norman.

      Lakeville, New Jersey.

      Shell Press, 1989.

      67 p.   Illus.

      Story of green turtle who eats green peas.

      1. Turtle Stories   I. Title   II. Author

Read these questions. Use the card to find the answers.

1. How many pages does the book have?   _____

2. Where was the book made?   _____

3. What is the call number?   _____

4. What is the subject?   _____

5. Is the book illustrated?   _____

6. What is the title?   _____

7. Where was the book made?   _____

8. Who is the publisher?   _____

9. What is the copyright date?   _____

10. What is the author's name?   _____

OVERVIEW—Catalog Card

Read the catalog card. Answer the questions. Remember all the answers are on the catalog card.

F Mystery of the Purple Balloon
St

String, Peter. Mystery of the Purple Balloon.

Stringtown, New Jersey: Air Press, 1989.

113 p. Illus.

1. Mystery I. Subject II. Author

---

1. What is the first line of the card? _____

2. Is the book illustrated? _____

3. When was the book made? _____

4. Where was the book made? _____

5. What is the title? _____

6. How many pages are in the book? _____

7. What is the call number? _____

8. What is the author's name? _____

9. Who is the publisher? _____

10. What is the book about? _____

11. What type of card is it? _____

WRITE YOUR OWN
SUBJECT CATALOG CARD
Pick a book of your choice to fill in the blanks.

Call
number

Subject

Title

Author

Place of publication and Publisher

Copyright Date

Pages

Illustrated or not

Sentence about what the book is about.

MAGAZINES

Children's magazines are an excellent tool for introducing young people to a variety of good literature. Magazines are both informative and entertaining and can be used to promote valuable reading and writing skills.

There are over eighty children's magazines. Some of these are specialized covering science, history, and astronomy; others are general in nature. Often children will pick up and read a magazine article or story when they are reluctant to read an entire book. Being able to select your own short stories and articles to read from a magazine of your choice can be a motivating factor for encouraging the reluctant reader.

Encourage students to read for pleasure by allowing a free time to choose and examine magazines. They will become familiar with different types of magazines and the content of those magazines by reading for pleasure.

Read stories and articles from a variety of magazines to the class.

Let your students take turns choosing and reading an item aloud to the class or to a small group.

WHAT MAGAZINE DO YOU NEED?

Do you know how to choose a magazine? Let's look at three magazine titles.

> Hamster World
> Dog News
> Cartoons Today

Which one would you choose to learn about hamsters? The answer is Hamster World.

Look at these magazine titles.

Hamster World	Cartoons Today
Skateboarding for Kids	Plays for Young People
Dog News	Poems for Young People
Football for Kids	Cats and Kids
Holidays Magazine	Dollhouse World

Answer these questions.

1. What magazine will help you learn about hamsters?

   _____

2. What magazine will help you learn about dogs?

   _____

3. What magazine will help you learn about your new skateboard?

   _____

WHAT MAGAZINE DO YOU NEED?

Do you know how to choose a magazine? Let's look at three magazine titles.

> Hamster World
> Dog News
> Cartoons Today

Which one would you choose to learn about hamsters? The answer is Hamster World.

Look at these magazine titles.

Hamster World	Cartoons Today
Skateboarding for Kids	Plays for Young People
Dog News	Poems for Young People
Football for Kids	Cats and Kids
Holidays Magazine	Dollhouse World

Answer these questions.

1. What magazine will help you set up your dollhouse?

   _____

2. What magazine will help you learn about football?

   _____

3. What magazine will help you learn about the next holiday?

   _____

WHAT MAGAZINE DO YOU NEED?

Do you know how to choose a magazine? Let's look at three magazine titles.

> Hamster World
> Dog News
> Cartoons Today

Which one would you choose to learn about hamsters? The answer is Hamster World.

Look at these magazine titles.

Hamster World	Cartoons Today
Skateboarding for Kids	Plays for Young People
Dog News	Poems for Young People
Football for Kids	Cats and Kids
Holidays Magazine	Dollhouse World

Answer these questions.

1. What magazine will help you learn about your favorite cartoon?

   _____

2. What magazine will help you learn about a play?

   _____

3. What magazine will help you learn about a poem?

   _____

USING MAGAZINE TABLE OF CONTENTS

Look at a magazine. The table of contents is in the front of the magazine. The titles of the stories are in the table of contents. The stories are also called the articles. You can find the title and page number of each article. The table of contents will tell you.

The table of contents will tell you many things. Short articles are listed. Special parts of the magazine are listed, too. You can find page numbers, too! Let's say that the magazine has a puzzle section. This will be listed in the table of contents too. You can find many things in the table of contents!

You can learn much about a magazine. Just look at the table of contents! It is your guide. It will help you learn about what is in the magazine.

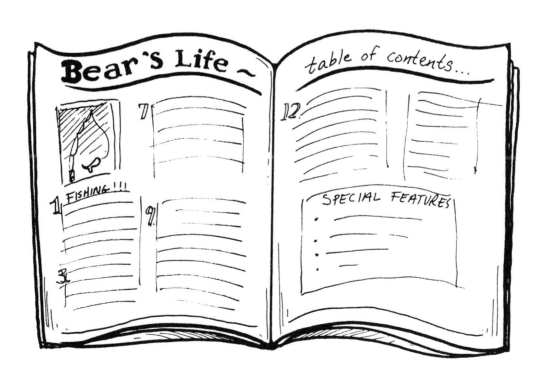

LET'S LOOK AT A TABLE OF CONTENTS

Story of Dogs
    by Joe Mark   page 3

Story of Cats
    by Mary Claw   page 5

Story of Birds
    by Jane Song   page 9

Copy the above chart on the blackboard so the children may look at it when they are asked the following questions.

Let's say you plan a report about birds. Can you find anything about birds in this magazine? Yes, you can. The title of this article is called "The Story of Birds."

Can you find the page this article starts on? Yes, you can. It starts on page nine. And, do you know who wrote it? Yes, you do. Jane Song wrote this article.

You see, a table of contents can help you!

Name _____

TABLE OF CONTENTS—The Magazine

Table of Contents

Reproduce this page for the children to use with pages 78 & 79.

NAME _____

TABLE OF CONTENTS—The Magazine
Use with reproducible chart on page 77.

Read the magazine table of contents. Use it to answer these questions.

1. How many stories are in this magazine? _____

2. On what page does "The Story of Green Plants" begin?

   _____

3. "The Story of Seeds" begins on page? _____

4. Can you find a story about how to grow plants? _____

5. What story did Joe Pot write?

   _____

6. What story did Jane Flower write?

   _____

7. Who wrote "How to Grow Big Flowers?"

   _____

TABLE OF CONTENTS—The Magazine

Use with reproducible chart on page 77.

Read the magazine table of contents. Use it to answer these questions.

1. Who wrote "Bugs in Your Garden?"

   _____

2. Who wrote "Sunshine and Your Garden?"

   _____

3. You will find puzzles on page? _____

4. You are writing a report about seeds. What is the title that may help you?

   _____

5. You are writing a report about how to grow plants and flowers. What two titles may help you?

   _____

   _____

6. You are writing a report about puzzles. What is the title that may help you?

   _____

USING THE MAGAZINE GUIDE

You can learn much from the magazine guide. It can help you find facts.

Let's say you plan a report. You can use magazines in your report. Remember, magazines have stories or articles. These articles give facts. And you can use facts for your reports.

But how do you find the articles in the magazine? You can use the magazine guide. What is the magazine guide? It tells you about magazine articles.

On the inside cover of the magazine guide is a list. It is a list of magazines. These are the magazines you can learn about in the guide.

What kind of information is in the guide? Let's look at part of the guide. This part is called the *entry*.

PLAY (1)

    Why Kids Need to Play. (2)

Robert Price. (3) Play Magazine

for Kids. (4)   April 1988. (5)   p. 14–17. (6)

1. **PLAY**—This part of the entry tells you the subject of the magazine article.

2. **Why Kids Need to Play?**—This is the title of the magazine article.

3. **Robert Price**—This is the writer of the magazine article.

4. **Play Magazine for Kids**—This is the name of the magazine.

5. **April 1988**—This is the date of the magazine.

6. **p. 14–17**—These are the pages of the magazine article.

USING THE MAGAZINE GUIDE

PETS: See also Dogs; fish; mice

Caring for Your Pet. Animal Magazine.

Dec. 1992. p. 10–15.

Finding Your Lost Pet. Pet Magazine.

November 1991. p. 6–9.

Fun Pets to Have. Dog and Pet

Magazine. October 1991. p. 3–6.

Silly Pet Stories. Story Magazine.

April 1992. p. 10–12.

Why Do People Have Pets?

Pet Magazine. January 1992. p. 4–9.

Reproduce this page for the children to use with page 82 & 83.

NAME _____

USING THE MAGAZINE GUIDE

Use with the reproducible chart on page 81.

The magazine guide has lists of articles. Use the guide to find what you need. It's a good tool. Let's learn how to use it. Use the entry for PETS to answer these questions.

1. How many magazine articles are listed here? _____

2. What is the title of the first article?   _____

3. What is the date of the first article?   _____

4. How many pages are in the first article? _____

5. On what page does the first article begin? _____

6. On what page does the first article end? _____

7. What is the title of the second article?   _____

8. What is the date of the second article?   _____

9. How many pages are in the second article? _____

USING THE MAGAZINE GUIDE

Use with the reproducible chart on page 81.

The magazine guide has lists of articles. Use the guide to find what you need. It's a good tool. Let's learn how to use it. Use the entry for PETS to answer these questions.

1. On what page does the second article begin? _____

2. You need to write a report about taking care of your pet.

    What article will help you? _____

3. You need to write a report about finding a lost pet.

    What article will help you? _____

4. Write the 5 magazine titles listed in this entry.

    (1) _____

    (2) _____

    (3) _____

    (4) _____

    (5) _____

USING THE MAGAZINE GUIDE

Using a magazine guide can be fun. You now know how to read a magazine entry. Now let's look at a part of the guide. Copy this chart on the blackboard and work together as a class to answer the following questions.

Dinosaurs and Their Food. Dinosaur

    Magazine. April 1991. p. 3–6

Dinosaurs and Their Feet. Dinosaur

    Magazine. October 1992. p. 4–5

Dinosaurs and Weather. Science

    Magazine. September 1992. p. 3–5

---

1. How many magazine articles are listed here? There are three magazine articles. They are:

   Dinosaurs and Their Food
   Dinosaurs and Their Feet
   Dinosaurs and Weather

2. How many magazines are listed here? _____

3. How many pages are in the magazine article "Dinosaurs and Their Food"? Look at pages 3–6. There are pages 3, 4, 5, and 6. This means there are four pages.

4. Can you learn about dinosaurs and their feet? Yes, you can. The title of the magazine article is "Dinosaurs and Their Feet."

5. Can you learn about dinosaurs and their eyes? No, there is not an article for this subject.

Now let's look at part of a magazine guide.

USING THE MAGAZINE GUIDE

PETS

Finding a Lost Pet. Mike Tail.

Pet Magazine. October 1990. p. 8–10.

Read the subject entry. Answer the questions below.

1. What is the subject of this entry? _____

2. What is the title of this article? _____

3. Who is the author of the article? _____

4. What is the title of the magazine? _____

5. What is the date of the magazine? _____

USING THE MAGAZINE GUIDE

Now look at the entry for animals.

```
ANIMALS
    Beavers and Their Homes.
Jane River. River Magazine.
September 1991. p. 3–5.
```

Read the subject entry for animals. Answer the questions below.

1. What is the subject of this entry?   _____

2. What is the title of this entry?   _____

3. Who is the author of the article?   _____

4. What is the title of the magazine?   _____

5. What is the date of the magazine?   _____

6. Look at the entry for animals. Can you use this magazine article to learn about birds?   _____

7. What can you learn about beavers?   _____

8. How many pages are in this article?   _____

NAME _____

MY FAVORITE MAGAZINE

1. Select a magazine from the class collection.

   Title: _____ Date: _____

2. Story/Article I liked best: _____

   Page number: _____

   Main character: _____

3. Study the magazine.
   List five different items found in the magazine.

   1. _____

   2. _____

   3. _____

   4. _____

   5. _____

4. What is your favorite part of the magazine? _____

   _____

   Why? _____

5. Think about the content of the magazine and write a new title for
   the magazine. _____

   Why did you choose this title? _____

   _____

6. Finish this sentence. Kids should read this magazine because

   _____

   _____

NAME _____

WHAT'S INSIDE OF A MAGAZINE?

Select one of the children's magazines from the class collection. Read and enjoy the magazine. Answer the following questions.

1. Magazine title _____ Issue Date_____

2. Number of pages _____

3. Number of fiction stories_____

   List the titles and page numbers _____

   _____

   _____

4. Number of nonfiction stories _____

   List the titles and page numbers _____

   _____

   _____

5. Does the magazine contain any of the following:
   Answer Yes or No   List the number found

   Poems _____   _____

   Craft projects_____   _____

   Puzzles _____   _____

   Letters to the Editor _____   _____

   Science articles _____   _____

   Biographies _____   _____

   Riddles _____   _____

   Jokes _____   _____

MARKET LIST

This market list is given only as a guide. There are many other magazines, newsletters, and quarterly publications that accept materials from young contributors. For an expanded and comprehensive listing, see the Young Writer's/Illustrator's market section of *Children's Writer's & Illustrator's Market* (Writer's Digest Books, 1992).

BOY'S LIFE
Box 152079
Irving, TX 75015-2079
    Fiction, nonfiction, poetry

CHILDREN'S ALBUM
Box 6086
Concord, CA 94524
    Fiction, artwork

CHILDREN'S DIGEST
Box 567
Indianapolis, IN 46206
    Fiction, poems, riddles, letters

CHILDREN'S PLAYMATE
Box 567
Indianapolis, IN 46206
    Poems, jokes, riddles, letters

CLUBHOUSE
Box 15
Berrien Springs, MI 49103
    Fiction, nonfiction, poetry,
    artwork

CREATIVE KIDS
Box 6448
Mobile, AL 36660
    Fiction, nonfiction, poetry, plays,
    artwork

HIGHLIGHTS FOR CHILDREN
803 Church Street
Honesdale, PA 18431
    Science letters, favorite books,
    recipes, special features, artwork

MERLYN'S PEN
Nation Magazine of Student Writing
Box 1058
East Grenwich, RI 02818
    Fiction, nonfiction, plays, letters
    to the editor, book reviews,
    artwork

MY FRIEND
50 St. Paul Avenue
Boston, MA 02130
    "Junior Reporter" features gives
    opportunity for students to sug-
    gest topics and do the research
    for an article.

PURPLE COW
3500 Piedmont Road NE, Suite 415
Atlanta, GA 30305
    Nonfiction, artwork

SCHOLASTIC SCOPE
730 Broadway
New, York, NY 10003
    Fiction, nonfiction, poetry

Market List—Continued

STONE SOUP
Box 83
Santa Cruz, CA 95063
   Fiction, poetry, artwork

STRAIGHT MAGAZINE
Standard Publishing
8121 Hamilton Avenue
Cincinnati, OH 45231
   Fiction, poetry, artwork

SUNSHINE MAGAZINE
Box 40
Sunshine Park
Litchfield, IL 62056
   Fiction, nonfiction, poetry

WOMBAT: A JOURNAL OF YOUNG PEOPLE'S WRITING AND ART
365 Ashton Drive
Athens, GA 30606
   Fiction, nonfiction, cartoons,
   puzzles, jokes, games, artwork

YOUNG VOICES MAGAZINE
P.O. Box 2321
Olympia, WA 98507
   Fiction, nonfiction, book reviews,
   poetry, artwork

CANADIAN MAGAZINES

CHICKADEE & OWL MAGAZINES
56 The Esplanade #304
Toronto, Ontario,
Canada M5E 1A7

RANGER RICK
Canadian Wildlife Federation
1673 Carling Ave.
Ottawa, Ontario
Canada K2A 3Z1

SOMEWHERE TODAY
Youth Editions
P.O. Box 1310, Station B
Hull, Quebec
Canada J8X 3Y1

TREE HOUSE
The Young Naturalist Foundation
56 The Esplanade #304
Toronto, Ontario,
Canada M5E 1A7

REFERENCE BOOKS

Reference books have a special purpose in the library. They are shelved in a special section of the library. They are used to get information for a report, to find an answer to a question, or to read about something in which you are interested.

A dictionary, a thesaurus, and an encyclopedia are examples of reference books.

The call number of a reference book has a capital "R" as part of it. This tells you that it is shelved in the reference section.

These books usually have a colored sign-out card. This tells you that borrowing is limited. Check with your librarian and teacher for the rules in your library.

THE ENCYCLOPEDIA

An encyclopedia is a set of books that contain information about many different subjects. Because the amount of information cannot all be put into one book, it is divided into many smaller books. Each book is called a volume.

The volumes in each set are arranged in alphabetical order to make it easy to find the information. They are also numbered to make it easy to keep them in order on the shelf.

On the pages, the subjects are arranged in alphabetical order with guide words on each page like a dictionary. To find a subject, look for the letter it begins with and choose that volume. Then spell the subject correctly and use the guide words to find it as you would do in a dictionary. The subjects are usually printed with large, dark letters.

To find a person, look for the person's last name.

To find a place named with two parts, look for the first part.

THE ENCYCLOPEDIA

Using Guide Letters

Below is a make-believe set of encyclopedias. Decide in which volume you would find the subjects listed. Write the guide letters in the blank space beside each subject.

A B C D E-F G H I-J-K L M N O P-Q R S T U-V W X-Y-Z INDEX

1. Horses _____

2. Trees _____

3. Daniel Boone _____

4. Elephants _____

9. New York _____

6. Laura Ingalls Wilder _____

7. Dogs _____

8. Mountains _____

9. Pennsylvania _____

10. Snakes _____

Taking Notes

The reason you find information is to take notes. Do not copy from the encyclopedia. Instead, pick out key words and write short phrases. Later you can use them to write your own sentences, adding the words you need to make complete sentences.

Giving the Source

• It is important to tell where you got your information. It gives credit to the person who first wrote it. It also proves that you looked up the information.

• The subjects you look under are called entries. The information which you read is called an article.

• The encyclopedia is a set.

• The volume you are using has certain letters. You are reading certain pages.

NAME _____

ENCYCLOPEDIA

Find a subject which you are assigned. Write it on the line below.

SUBJECT ASSIGNED _____

Write some information about the subject. Do not copy from the article. Instead, write some key words in short phrases. Later you can use them to write your own sentences for a report.

_____

_____

_____

_____

_____

Tell where you found it by filling in the blanks below.

1. The title of the article is the heading of what you will read. It is usually in darker print on the page of the encyclopedia.

2. The encyclopedia is the name on the cover.

3. The volume is the letter on the spine.

4. The pages are the ones you will read.

Source of information

1. _____   2. _____
      Title of the Article   Encyclopedia

2. _____   4. _____
         Volume   Pages

THE DICTIONARY

The dictionary is a book of words listed alphabetically. For each word, a dictionary gives you the correct spelling and tells you what the word means. A dictionary also shows you how to say, or pronounce a word, and how the word can be used in a sentence. Sometimes the dictionary will have pictures to help describe unfamiliar nouns.

bake   beach

bake (bak) To cook in an oven. Mom will bake a cake.

balloon (bal-loon) A toy made of thin rubber that you can blow up with air. I bought a baloon at the circus.

barn (bärn) A building on a farm. The cows are in the barn.

baseball (bas-bal) A game played with a ball and a bat. A baseball team has nine players.

beach (bech) Land next to water. My family goes to the beach in the summer.

bear   bell

bear (bar) A large shaggy animal. The bear ran out of the woods.

bedtime (bed-tim) The time you go to sleep. My bedtime is 9:00.

believe (be-leve) To think something is true. I believe the story in the book.

bell (bel) Something that rings. Did you hear the school bell ring?

NAME _____

GUIDE WORDS

Guide words are found at the top of each page in a dictionary. These words are helpful because they tell you the first and last entry words on a page – they will "guide" you to all the entry words in between them. Look up the following words in a dictionary and write the two guide words that you find on the top of the page.

1. mountain　　_____　　_____

2. cotton　　_____　　_____

3. lion　　_____　　_____

4. umbrella　　_____　　_____

5. picture　　_____　　_____

6. yellow　　_____　　_____

7. butterfly　　_____　　_____

8. queen　　_____　　_____

9. kite　　_____　　_____

10. honey　　_____　　_____

USING A DICTIONARY

A dictionary can be used to check spelling or to find out if a word should be capitalized. Look up the following words in a dictionary.
- If the word is misspelled, spell it correctly.
- If a word needs to have a capital letter, write it with a capital.
- If the word appears to be correct, write "correct."

1. tuesday _____

2. handkercheif _____

3. christmas _____

4. speling _____

5. november _____

6. brothor _____

7. knowledge _____

8. germany _____

9. autum _____

10. president _____

WHAT IS A BIOGRAPHY?

What is a *biography*? A biography tells the true story of a person's life. Let's say Peter Rockwell tells the true story of George Washington. This is called a biography. Let's look at another example. Let's say James Jones wrote the true story of Abe Lincoln. This is also called a biography.

How do you find a biography on the library shelf? You need to know its call number. How do you make a call number for a biography? Use the number 921. But how do we know who the story is about? Look under 921. There will be two letters. These letters come from the last name of the person the book is about.

How do you make a call number for the biography by Peter Rockwell? First, write 921. Then write Wa for Washington. The call number looks like this:

| 921
Wa | The number 921 tells you it is a biography. |

The letters Wa tell you the book is about Washington.

How would you write a call number for the book about Abe Lincoln? Write 921 and Li:

| 921
Li |

NAME _____

IS IT A BIOGRAPHY?

Read each book title below. Is it a biography? If it is, write "biography." If it is not, write "No."

1. *The True Story of Benjamin Franklin* _____

2. *Rocks and Shells* _____

3. *Life on the Prairie* _____

4. *The Life of President Kennedy* _____

5. *Stars, Planets, and Space* _____

6. *The Story of Martin Luther King* _____

7. *Bees, Wasps, and Insects* _____

8. *People of India* _____

9. *How to Take Care of Your Puppy* _____

10. *Life of Laura Ingalls Wilder* _____

11. *Famous Movie Stars* _____

12. *Sport Stars: Their Stories* _____

13. *The Exciting Lives of Rock Stars* _____

14. *Presidents: Their Lives* _____

15. *Insects* _____

IS IT A BIOGRAPHY?

Read the book titles below. Is it a biography? If it is, write "biography." If it is not, write "No."

1. *The Life of a Ladybug* _____

2. *Life of Abraham Lincoln* _____

3. *Dr. Seuss: Famous Author* _____

4. *Purple Kites* _____

5. *The Life of a Hamster* _____

6. *The Life of a Cat* _____

7. *Life of George Washington* _____

8. *Walt Disney: His Story* _____

9. *Benjamin Franklin: His Life* _____

10. *The Davy Crockett Story* _____

11. *Daniel Boone: His Life* _____

12. *Dog Stories* _____

13. *Baseball Stories* _____

14. *Horse Stories* _____

15. *Life of Johnny Appleseed* _____

NAME _____

Write a biography about someone you admire.

_____

_____

_____

_____

_____

_____

_____

_____

_____

_____

_____

_____

WHAT IS AN AUTOBIOGRAPHY AND A COLLECTIVE BIOGRAPHY?

Not all books about people are called biographies.

An **autobiography** also tells the true story of a person's life. But the person writes the story himself or herself.

Sometimes more than one biography is in one book. A writer may collect the biographies and put them in one book. This is called a **collective biography.**

Let's look at each of these types of books. Let's say Walt Disney wrote about his life. He tells what it is like to make cartoons. This is called an **autobiography**. If someone else wrote about his life this would be called a **biography.**

If Walt Disney and the life stories of other cartoon writers are all in one book this would be called a **collective biography.**

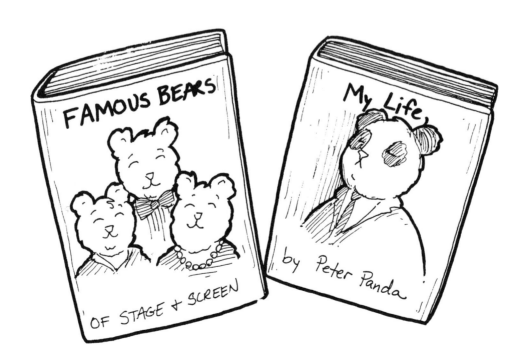

IS IT AN AUTOBIOGRAPHY OR BIOGRAPHY?

Write biography, autobiography or "neither" for each book title.

1. *The Life of E.B. White* by Rosa Spider.   _____

2. *A Writer's Life: Laura Ingalls Wilder*
   by Laura Ingalls Wilder.   _____

3. *Insects* by Arthor C. Bugg   _____

4. *Pocohantas: Her Story* by Rachal Jones   _____

5. *Indians of America* by T.R. Crow   _____

6. *Poems, Stories, and Plays* by C.W. Writer   _____

7. *How to Choose a Cookbook* by R.T. Book   _____

8. *My Life in Television* by George Famous   _____

9. *Martin Luther King: My Story*
   by Martin Luther King   _____

10. *Spiders and their Webs* by C.C. Web   _____

NAME _____

WRITING CALL NUMBERS FOR BIOGRAPHY BOOKS

Write a call number for each biography.

1. *The Story of Abraham Lincoln*

   by Ted Log

2. *The Life of Johnny Appleseed*

   by Sandia Seed

3. *The Life of Davy Crockett*

   by Robert Woods

4. *The Life of George Washington*

   by Cherry Tree

5. *Thomas Jefferson: His Story*

   by William President

Can you put these call numbers in order?

BIOGRAPHY LIBRARY ORDER

Put the call numbers in order.

Autobiography

921 Da	921 Ba	921 Ca	921 Wa	921 Ra

_____ _____ _____ _____ _____

Biography

921 Se	921 Wa	921 Ro	921 Za	921 Wr

_____ _____ _____ _____ _____

Collective Biography

920 Tr	920 Ca	920 Ab	920 Gr	920 Ha

_____ _____ _____ _____ _____

Write the words "collective biography"
after each call number that is a collective biography.

921 Ba	_____	920 Ca	_____
902 Tr		920 Tu	

NAME _____

COLLECTIVE BIOGRAPHY
Write the title of the collective biography for each group.

The Book of Presidents   **The Book of Famous Astronauts**

The Book of Writers   **Lives of Sport Stars**

1. Thomas Jefferson
   George Washington
   Abraham Lincoln

   _____

2. Laura Ingalls Wilder
   E.B. White
   Beverly Cleary

   _____

3. Babe Ruth
   Micky Mantle
   Willie Mays

   _____

4. Sally Ride
   John Glen
   Neil Armstrong

   _____

Write the call numbers.

1. *Book Presidents* by T.H. Office

2. *Book of Famous Americans* by R.R. History

3. *Lives of Sport Stars* by S.S. Sunshine

COLLECTIVE BIOGRAPHY CALL NUMBERS

Write the call number for each collective biography.

1. *The Lives of Writers*

   by C.W. Word

2. *Famous Women in History*

   by T.R. Tell

3. *Musicians of Today*

   by R.A. Note

4. *Astronauts*

   by J.J. Space

5. *Artists and Their Paintings*

   by T.T. Brush

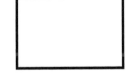

Put these call numbers in order.

| 920 Ca | 920 To | 920 Ab | 920 Br | 920 Ho |

_____ _____ _____ _____ _____

POETRY

Poetry is a special kind of writing that makes you feel a certain way. Sometimes it makes you laugh and giggle until you can't stop. Other poetry sings like music. Some poems are very serious – they might make you cry, or they might send a shiver down your spine.

The main difference between poetry and other writing is that poetry makes you see and feel more than other writing does. Poetry does not explain or tell you about something as much as it seems to ask you to join in.

Nursery rhymes, nonsense, and humorous poems are the most popular forms of children's poetry.

Nursery rhymes are most often associated with Mother Goose.

Mother Goose Activities
- Look in a Mother Goose book and memorize a short rhyme for the class.

- Brainstorm as a class, and make a list of all the rhymes the children already know.

Nonsense poems are poems with little or no meaning at all – sometimes even the words of these poems have no meaning. The following are good sources of nonsense poetry.

A Book of Nonsense Songs and Stories by Edward Lear.

Tirra Lirra, Rhymes of Old and New by Laura Richards.

Humorous poetry is like nonsense poetry, except humorous poetry deals with events that could possibly happen to a person or an animal. Below are some good sources for humorous poetry.

Hurry, Hurray, Mary Dear! by N.M. Bodecker.
Snowman Sniffles and Other Verse by N.M. Bodecker.
The Little Father by Gelett Burgess.
Jabberwocky by Lewis Caroll.
Doodle Soup by John Ciardi.
Fast and Slow: Poems for Advanced Children of Beginning Parents
    by John Ciardi.
Poem Stew (A collection of poetry) edited by William Cole.
The Skylighters by Graeme and Neil Canning.
Brats by X. J. Kennedy
Ghastlies, Goons & Pincushions: Nonsense Verse by X. J. Kennedy
The Jumblies by Edward Lear.
The Owl and the Pussycat by Edward Lear.
The Scroobious Pip by Edward Lear.

Other well-known children's poets:

Byrd Baylor
Nikki Giovanni
James Houston
Karla Kuskin
Myra Cohn Livingston
David McCord
Eve Merriam
Jack Prelutsky
Maurice Sendak
Shel Silverstein
Judith Viorst

THE LIMERICK

The limerick is a type of nonsense verse with a five-line format. The first and second lines rhyme together, the third and fourth lines rhyme together, and the last line rhymes with the first two. These are good places to find limericks:

The Hopeful Trout and Other Limericks by John Ciardi.
The Book of Pigericks: Pig Limericks by Arnold Lobel.
Laughable Limericks (Sara and John Brewton, comps)
Lots of Limericks (Myra Cohn Livingston, comp)
*They've Discovered a Head in the Box for the Bread and Other
    Laughable Limericks* (John Brewton and Lorraine Blackburn,
    comps)

Here are some fun limericks, all written by unknown authors, that will be fun to read to your class.

BALLET
A hippo decided one day
That she would take up ballet,
    So she stood on her toes
    And said, "Okay, here goes!"
And fell back with a splash in the bay.

A SHAGGY DOG
There was a small maiden named Maggie,
Whose dog was enormous and shaggy,
    The front end of him
    Looked vicious and grim —
But the tail end was friendly and waggy.

SPELL IT

You have to be brainy, not drippy,
To learn how to spell Mississippi.
    The i's, p's and s's
    Take knowing, not guesses.
I think they are meant to be trippy.

A YOUNG LADY OF CRETE

There was a young lady of Crete,
Who was so exceedingly neat.
    When she got out of bed
    She stood on her head,
To make sure of not soiling her feet.

GOOD THINKING

There was, in the village of Patton
A chap who at church kept his hat on.
    "If I wake up," he said,
    "With my hat on my head,
"I'll know that it hasn't been sat on."

AN OLD MAN FROM PERU

There was an old man from Peru
Who dreamed he was eating his shoe.
    He awoke in the night
    And turned on the light
And found it was perfectly true.

A YOUNG LADY NAMED SUE

There was a young lady named Sue,
Who wanted to catch the 2:02;
    Said the trainman, "Don't hurry
    Or flurry or worry;
It's a minute or two to 2:02."

THE CARELESS ZOOKEEPER

A careless zookeper named Blake
Fell into a tropical lake.
    Said a fat alligator
    A few minutes later,
"Very nice, but I still prefer steak."

FREE VERSE

Poetry does not always make you laugh; some poetry was written to make you think about something in a new way, or to show you something you hadn't noticed before.

Free verse is a type of poetry that does not always rhyme. Many times when you hear free verse read to you, you do not notice anything special about it, but when you see it written on the page you can understand it better. Often the words themselves take on an interesting form.

Here are some fun free verse books:
Small Poems by Valerie Worth
Silvehorn: The Hilda Conkling Book for Other Children
    by Hilda Conkling

Here are some examples of free verse to show the children in your class. Have the children try to create some free verse of their own.

THE SNAKE IS HIDING IN THE ROCKS, WATCH OUT !!!!

It
is
raining.   Raining
            down
                on
                    me .

I Like to play Ball. Bounce Bounce Bounce Bounce

NATURE POEMS

Many serious poems (poems that are not humorous) are written about the beauty of nature. These are called nature poems. Below are some good places to find nature poems.

Crickets and Bullfrogs and Whispers of Thunder: Poems by Harry Behn.

The Sacred Path: Spells, Prayers, and Power of the American Indians by John Bierhorst.

When it Comes to Bugs: Poems by Aillen Fisher.

I Am Phoenix: Poems for Two Voices by Paul Fleischman.

Joyful Noise: Poems for Two Voices by Paul Fleischman.

Moonsong Lullaby by Jamake Highwater.

The Sky is Full of Song by Lee Bennett Hopkins.

A Circle of Seasons by Myra Cohn Livingston.

Earth Songs by Myra Cohn Livingston.

River Winding by Charlotte Zolotow.

Read the children some nature poems. Have them close their eyes and try to visualize the words that they are listening to. Ask the children to illustrate a picture to accompany their favorite nature poem.

FANTASY

When you read a fantasy, you step into a strange, new world of make-believe people, places and things. Writers make many different types of worlds. Some of these worlds you know very well. The mystery story, the science fiction story, and the fantasy story are just a few of these made-up worlds.

What is the world of fantasy? In this type of story strange things can happen and often do. People say or do things differently than you might expect. And the settings of these stories are not the everyday places you know.

Let's say the doors of your school bus opened. You step off and stand before the school. What do you see? The school walls are no longer brick, but made of candy. The doors have large red gumdrops as door knobs. And the ceiling lights are licorice strands. This world can not be explained. Let's go on. There is a striped zebra in each classroom. And there are teddy bears at each desk. Strange places, strange characters, and strange happenings. This is the world of fantasy.

THE FANTASY STORY

One crisp morning as you are getting ready for school the strangest thing happens. You walk to the refrigerator to get your orange juice and butter for your toast. As you open the door, a bright orange begins to chat.

"Good morning," he says. And he waves his large top hat and rubs his two black button eyes. "I am looking for the lemon and lime but I just can not seem to find them."

Well, you quickly close the door. Can this really be happening? Your first thought is to leave but your curiosity has the better of you. And so you open the door.

"As I was saying," continues the orange, and as he continues to talk you can not help notice that his tennis shoes are just a bit too big for his feet. "It is very important that I find the lemon and lime for I must gather all the important fruits to begin the first annual fruit parade."

As you blink your eyes you notice that all the fruits are lining up each one looking for a good spot on the parade line. The blueberries are lining up next to the cherries and the pineapple is taking the lead. It must be because of his magnificent headdress you think.

This is a fantasy story. Why? Well, obviously the fruits in a refrigerator can not line up and begin to organize their own annual fruit parade. Or can they? Can pineapples lead a parade? Can an orange wear tennis shoes that are just a bit too big for him?

And yet, in a fantasy story you are asked to do just that—suspend your ideas you might have about the world. And prepare to accept a new world as it is presented to you—no questions asked. Can you do that? That is what fantasy stories ask you to do. A fantasy story creates a world on its own terms. Characters, settings, and happenings do not have to be explained. They just are—they exist on their own terms.

A fantasy story can take place anywhere at any time and with any characters. Characters are often strange and different.

There are several types of fantasy stories. You are probably familiar with some already. Every time you read a ghost story you are reading a fantasy. When you read a fable or fairy tale you are entering the world of fantasy. And do not forget the myth. This is a fantasy too.

FANTASY ACTIVITIES:

1. You have just arrived at school and it is made of a huge cracker. The doors are huge chocolate bars and the drinking fountains are filled with soda. Tell us what happens next...

2. Read a fantasy story. Tell what makes it a fantasy.

3. A fantasy story of your choice is going to be made into a movie. How would you promote it? Draw your ideas. You may use poster paper so that your advertisement can be seen easily from a distance.

4. Draw a fantasy poster. Choose a favorite fantasy story character to include on your poster.

5. Write your own fantasy. You are in the kitchen. You hear a noise. Suddenly, the refrigerator comes alive. It begins to talk to you. What does it say? What does it do? What does it look like?

FANTASIES FOR THIRD GRADERS

BEAST TALES

The Mushroom Center Disaster by N.M. Bodecker
The Roquerort Gang by Sandy Clifford
Zucchini by Barbara Dana
Lesse Webster by Ursula Le Guin
Hugh Pine by Janwillem Van de Wetering

ALTERNATE WORLDS

The Truthful Harp by Lloyd Alexander
Quimble Wood by N.M. Bodecker
The Brownies: Their Book by Palmer Cox
Coll and His White Pig by Lloyd Alexander

HUMOROUS

The Acorn Quest by Jane Yolen
Sleeping Ugly by Jane Yolen
Baby Island by Carol Ryrie Brink
All the Money in the World by Bill Brittain
The Devil and Mother Crump by Valerie Soho
Sebastian (Super-Sleuth) and the Crummy Yummies Caper
    by Blount Christian

TIME TRAVEL

Parsley, Sage, Rosemary and Time by Jane Louise Curry
The Mysterious Girl in the Garden by Judith St. George
Mighty Magic: An Almost-True Story of Pirates and Indians
    by Selden M. Loring

TOYS

The Adventures of Jack Ninepins by Esther Averill
Miss Hickory by Carolyn Sherwin Baily
Jeeter, Mason and the Magic Headset by Maggie Twohill
When the Dolls Woke by Marjorie Filley Stover
Winnie-the-Pooh by A.A. Milne
Jumanji by Chris Van Allsburg

FAIRY TALES

Every country has stories that are so old, people cannot remember where they came from. These old stories have been kept alive because they have been told over and over throughout history. These stories that we know as fairy tales have come from three major places: France, Germany, and Denmark.

Charles Perrault and his son Pierre, who were Frenchmen, were the first to actually collect the fairy tales they knew and write them down. The Perraults are especially well known for these familiar tales that were recorded three hundred years ago.

Cinderella
Little Red Riding Hood
Sleeping Beauty
Puss in Boots
Blue Beard
The Goose Girl
The Frog Prince
The Bremen Town Musicians

The Grimm Brothers, Jacob and Wilhelm, lived in Germany and began to collect stories that were important to their German tradition and language. Many, many years before the Grimm brothers were even born the stories they collected had been told in castles and cottages throughout Germany. A few of the most popular stories these brothers wrote down include:

Hansel and Gretel
Snow White and the Seven Dwarfs
Rapunzel
The Elves and the Shoemaker
Rumpelstiltskin

Hans Christian Andersen, from Denmark, is known for his wide collection of stories and for writing them as well. Unlike the Perraults or the Grimm Brothers, Hans Christian Andersen actually made up his stories himself. Many of the stories he wrote come from his own experiences.

He was a thin man with large feet and a large nose – he had firsthand experience knowing what it felt like to be an "Ugly Duckling." Hans was born into a poor but happy family. His father, who was a shoemaker, told Hans many stories and even built Hans his own puppet theatre.

Although Hans Christian Andersen did not believe his stories were as good as his other writing, he wrote a new fairy tale each Christmas for children of all ages. The following stories are a few of Hans Christian Andersen's most famous stories:

The Ugly Duckling
Thumbelina
The Princess and the Pea
The Emperor's New Clothes
The Little Mermaid
The Steadfast Tin Soldier
The Little Match Girl

FABLE

A fable is one of the oldest types of stories ever told. Why? People like to learn. Often, a community needs to teach lessons. Teaching important lessons in life can be done by telling a story.

The fable is a story that teaches. This type of story teaches lessons about how to live. Often, these lessons are called morals of the stories. The characters in these stories learn. And the community that tells these stories learns.

Fables are short tales in which animals speak and act like human beings. The characters in fables are not given their own names – they are simply called "rabbit," "fox," or "hare," – or the name of whatever animal they are representing.

Most fables originated in the country of Greece over two thousand years ago. These fables are thought to have been written by a man named Aesop. A French poet named La Fountaine is also well known for his poetic fables which were derived from the fables of Aesop. A third major source of fables comes from the country of India. The Panchatantra, which means "five books," and the Jatakas (two or three thousand stories) are both large collections of Indian fables that were written in a folktale style.

Listed below are ten of Aesop's fables. Look up one of them in the library, read it, and write what you think is the moral, or meaning of the story.

The Lion and the Fox   *The Wolf and His Shadow*
The Fox and the Grapes   *The Frog and the Ox*
The Tortoise and the Hare   *The Dog and the Shell*
The Lion and the Mouse   *The Cat and the Mouse*
The Cicada and the Ants   *The Fox and the Crow*

FABLE ANIMALS

Reproduce the animals. Ask the children to choose two animals. Have them color and cut-out their animals and then write their own fable about the animals.

FABLE ANIMALS

The animals in fables were given qualities in order to teach a moral. For example, the lion was always a powerful or kingly character, whereas the fox always had a sly and crafty personality. Draw an animal that you think has a human quality about it. (Ideas: raccoon, shark, snake, turtle, kitten, lamb, etc.) Be sure to include the "human quality" in your drawing.

THE PLAY

Sometimes we can read a story as a play. A play is a special type of story. You learn what happens in a story because the characters tell what happens and talk to each other.

A play does not have chapters as a book does. It has acts. An *act* is like a chapter in a book. It divides the play into parts. A play can have one, two, or even three acts. Usually the acts are broken down into *scenes*. There can be many scenes in one act. Just before you read the first act, you will see a list of characters. This list tells you who the characters are. The people who play the characters are called the *cast*. Look at the example below. It will show you what a list of characters will look like:

Mr. Tucker, a shopkeeper in Boston
Josh, clerk in the shop
Jacob Kemper, an artist
Cal, clerk in the shop
Sarah, Mr. Tucker's daughter
Irene, the maid
Mr. Samson, friend of Mr. Tucker
Mrs. Samson, friend of Mr. Tucker
Trina, the Samson's daughter

After the list of characters you will see a few sentences about where and when the play takes place. This is called the *setting*. Look below.

It is two days before the Christmas of 1928 and Mr. Tucker is in his shop talking with his two shop clerks before closing. Snow is gently falling.

In order to put on a play, the cast needs a *director*. A director has the job of guiding and teaching the actors how to perform on a stage. In addition to the actors, a play may also have a *narrator*, who is also part of the play. The narrator explains to the audience what is happening or what is about to happen. A narrator is helpful in a play if the audience needs background information to understand the play.

Have you ever been in a play? If you have, tell the class about the play. What was the name of the play? What part did you play? Was there a large cast? Would you ever like to be in a play?

Here is a list of plays that third graders will enjoy:

Small Plays for Special Days by Sue Alexander.
Paddington on Stage by Alfred Bradely and Micheal Bond.
James and the Giant Peach: The Play by Roald Dahl.
Year-Round Programs for Young Players by Aileen Fisher.
*Plays from Favorite Folk Tales: 25 One-Act Dramatizations of
    Stories Children Love* edited by Sylvia Kamerman.
Everyday Plays for Girls and Boys by Helen Miller.

THE PLAY

1. Draw illustrations to advertise this play. Remember, your posters will be introducing the play.

2. Pick a character from the play. Draw a poster showing what you think the character is like.

3. Rewrite the ending of the play. Write the ending as you would like to read it. Or if you like the ending, tell why you think it is a good ending.

PLAY VOCABULARY

If you ever spend time on a stage with actors and a stage crew while they are preparing for a play, you would probably hear words like this:

apron – the very front part of a stage that extends out beyond the curtain.

backdrop – large pieces of cloth that are painted with scenery and hung at the rear of the stage.

flat – a piece of wood or cardboard that is painted and stands upright on the stage as a piece of scenery or the wall of a room.

props (properties) – objects used by the actors in a play.

rehearsal – a practice going through the play slowly to find out where the actors will stand, when they will come on and off the stage, etc.

dress rehearsal – is a practice in full costume. There are no breaks as the play is presented as if for an audience.

script – the written-out version of a play. The script has all of the actors' lines, as well as directions for how the actors should move and how the scenery should look.

SUGGESTED AUTHORS FOR THIRD GRADE

ANIMALS
Aardema, Verna
Potter, Beatrice
Yolen, Jane

SCHOOL
Cleary, Beverly
Giff, Patricia
Hurwitz, Johanna
Parish, Peggy
Sharmat, Marjorie
Stolz, Mary

FANTASY
Cosgrove, Steven

HISTORICAL FICTION
Bulla, Robert Clyde
Dagliesch, Alice
Fritz, Jean
MacLaughlan, Patricia

MYSTERY
Adler, David
Levy, Elizabeth
Troll, Easy-To-Read Mysteries

POETRY
Cole, William
Pomerantz, Charlotte
Prelutsky, Jack
Viorst, Judith

GLOSSARY

1. **autobiography**—If the person tells the story him/herself it is called an autobiography.

2. **author card**—The author card begins with the author's last name. It is always the first line on the card.

3. **book pocket**—The book pocket is usually at the back of the book. It holds the library charge out card. And it will have the call number on it.

4. **book spine**—The book spine is the edge of a book. This is what you see when you pull a book from the shelves. You will find the call number on the spine.

5. **call number**—This number is on the spine of the book, book pocket, and library charge out card. It tells you where you can find a library book. Under the capital letter F, you will find the first two letters of the author's last name. The letter F stands for fiction.

6. **catalog card**— This card tells who wrote the book, title of the book, publisher, copyright date, illustrations, and number of pages in the book.

7. **catalog card drawers**—The card catalog is made of catalog drawers. On the outside of each drawer are letters. These letters tell you the catalog cards in the drawer. For example, a drawer letters A–C has cards A, B, and C.

8. **collective biography**—Sometimes more than one biography is put in one book. Then it is called a collective biography.

9. **copyright date**—This date is like the birth date of the book. It is the date the book was introduced to the public.

10. *fiction*—Fiction books tell you about people, places, or things. These stories are not true.

11. *illustration*—Illustrations are the pictures in the book.

12. *index*—An index is a list of subjects that are in the book. It is in alphabetical order. It is at the back of the book.

13. *library charge out card*—This card is in the library book pocket. It has the name of the book on it. The librarian holds this card until you return your book.

14. *magazine*—A magazine is a short collection of stories or articles. It usually appears once a month.

15. *nonfiction*—A nonfiction book tells a true story. The story is based upon facts. There are many kinds of nonfiction books.

16. *publisher*—The publisher is the group of people who make the book. They print it and put it together.

17. *subject*—This is what the book is about.

18. *subject card*—The subject card begins with the subject, always in capital letters.

19. *table of contents*—A table of contents tells you the title of each chapter in the book. It is at the front of the book. A table of contents in the magazine tells you the names of the articles or stories in the magazine.

20. *title card*—The title card begins with the title of the book. It is always the first line on the card.